WILD about YOU

A 60-DAY DEVOTIONAL FOR COUPLES

WILD
about
YOU

A 60-DAY DEVOTIONAL FOR COUPLES

JOHN AND STASI ELDREDGE

NELSON
BOOKS

An Imprint of Thomas Nelson

INTRODUCTION

*M*arriage is wild—we have to begin here. Sometimes it's wonderful and sometimes it's awful, but what makes it truly wild is the reality that you have been entrusted with the heart of another human being. Whatever else your life's great mission will entail, loving and defending this heart next to you is part of your great quest.

The hope of this couple's devotional is to bring to your marriage new understanding and, with that understanding, compassion for one another. Which we believe will bring new hope! This devotional gathers passages from *Captivating* and *Wild at Heart* and provides an opportunity for daily introspection and a deeper understanding of your spouse. It is an opportunity to rekindle the flame and perhaps even be wild about each other again!

These sixty short devotions gracefully blend Scripture verses, prayers, and thought-provoking questions designed to draw you closer together and help you discover who God created both of you to be.

There are two devotions per day, one focused on women and one focused on men. Reading both will help you get to know one another better than ever before, strengthen your faith together, and rediscover your love and passion for one another.

Remember that this is a couple's devotional and is designed to be used together. Try reading it aloud to one another. Then answer the questions together. Close your time by praying together, using the prayers as a springboard for your own conversation with God.

Another way to use this book is to read it daily as an individual, write down your thoughts, and then meet with your spouse to discuss your insights and findings.

Caring for our hearts isn't selfishness; it's how we begin to love. No matter what season of life and love you and your spouse are currently journeying through, these devotions have something for you. We pray this is the go-to devotional resource for you to get (and stay!) wild about one another. Let your journey to hope and healing begin today. May your marriage become a sanctuary for each other's hearts!

about HER

She is clothed with strength and dignity.

PROVERBS 31:25.

e were camping in the Tetons and the air was cool, fragrant with pine and sage, and the swiftly moving river beckoned. As we drifted toward the bank, a bull moose rose from the tall grasses, exactly where we had planned to come ashore. He was huge. He was gorgeous. He was in the way. Blocking the only exit we had. Remarkable speed, seventeen hundred pounds of muscle and antlers, and total unpredictability make moose dangerous indeed. It would take about two seconds for him to hit the water running and capsize our canoe. We could not pass. The mood changed. John and I were worried. There was only one alternative to this way out, now closed to us, and that was paddling back upriver in what had become total darkness. Silently, soberly, we turned the canoe and headed up, searching for the right channel that would keep us out of the main current. We hadn't planned on the adventure taking that turn, but suddenly, everything was required. John must steer with skill; I must paddle with strength. One mistake on our part and the strong current would force the canoe broadside, fill it, and sweep our boys off downriver into the night. It was glorious. We did it. He did. I did. We rose to the challenge working together, and the fact that it required all of me—that I was in it with my family and for my family, that I was surrounded by wild, shimmering beauty and it was, well, kind of *dangerous*—made the time transcendent. I was no longer Stasi. I was Sacagawea, Native American Princess of the West, a valiant and strong woman.

....

Jesus, teach me to be valiant and strong, a woman who embraces the adventures you have prepared for me.

A man's heart reveals the man.

PROVERBS 27:19 NKJV

Though the tracks I found this morning were fresh, that holds little promise. A bull elk can easily cover miles of rugged country in no time. He is one of the most elusive creatures we have left in the lower forty-eight. They are the ghost kings of the high country, more cautious and wary than deer, and more difficult to track. They live at higher elevations and travel farther in a day than nearly any other game. The bulls especially seem to carry a sixth sense to human presence. A few times I've gotten close; the next moment they are gone, vanishing silently into aspen groves so thick you wouldn't have believed a rabbit could get through. It wasn't always this way. For centuries elk lived out on the prairies, grazing together on the rich grasses in vast numbers. Meriwether Lewis described passing herds lolling about in the thousands as he made his way in search of a Northwest Passage. But by the end of the century, westward expansion had pushed the elk high up into the Rocky Mountains. Now they are elusive, hiding out at timberline like outlaws. If you would seek them now, it is on their terms, in forbidding haunts well beyond the reach of civilization. And that is why I come. And why I linger here still, letting the old bull get away. My hunt, you see, actually has little to do with elk. I knew that before I came. There is something else I am after, out here in the wild. I am searching for an even more elusive prey—something that can only be found through the help of wilderness. I am looking for my heart.

....

Dear Heavenly Father, I trust that you have already provided ways for me to reconnect with you and with my heart through nature.

Where have I failed to embrace my strength?

_____

_____

_____

Where are you calling me to be strong?

_____

_____

_____

Has your experience been largely suburban? How have you
tasted this life in the wild?

_____

_____

_____

On this journey to find your heart, where are you today?

_____

_____

_____

about HER

> *"Daughter, your faith has healed you. Go in*
> *peace and be freed from your suffering."*
>
> MARK 5:34

I love the story in Mark 5 of the woman with the issue of blood who, out of *her* desperate need, pushes through the throngs of people surrounding Jesus in order to touch the hem of his garment and be healed. She had been bleeding for twelve years. She had spent all she had on the many doctors and treatments available to her. None of it had helped. In fact, she had only gotten worse. Now, broke and heartbroken, she has an unlooked-for opportunity. Jesus has come to her town. It is not lawful for her, a bleeding woman, to be gathered with other people. But she is dying. And she doesn't want to be. So against all odds and against the law, she presses *through* the crowd and presses *in* to Jesus. She reaches out with all the strength she yet possesses and touches him and is instantly healed. Wow. Let that sink in for just a moment. She is instantly *healed*. This story is one of the lost treasures of the gospel. The Bible tells us that Jesus never changes. "Jesus Christ is the same yesterday, today and forever" (Hebrews 13:8). Jesus still has the power to heal us as women, to touch *us*, to restore us in our places of deepest need. And we all have need. All of us. In fact, some of us have been bleeding much longer than twelve years. Where have you lost hope? What do you need to press into Jesus for? Ask Jesus to come for *your* heart. He loves to do that. In fact, it is why he came.

....

Jesus, I put my trust in you because you love me. I open myself to you and welcome you to come for my heart.

God called to him from within the bush, "Moses! Moses!"

EXODUS 3:4

dventure, with all its requisite danger and wildness, is a deeply spiritual longing written into the soul of man. The masculine heart needs a place where nothing is digital, modular, nonfat, or online. Where there are no deadlines, smartphones, or committee meetings. Where there is room for the soul. Where, finally, the geography around us corresponds to the geography of our heart. Look at the heroes of the biblical text: Moses does not encounter the living God at the mall. He finds him (or is found by him) somewhere out in the deserts of Sinai, a long way from the comforts of Egypt. Where did the great prophet Elijah go to recover his strength? To the wild. As did John the Baptist, and his cousin Jesus, who was led by the Spirit into the wilderness. Whatever else those explorers were after, they were also searching for themselves.

Deep in a man's heart are some fundamental questions that simply cannot be answered at the kitchen table. *Who am I? What am I made of? What am I destined for?* It is fear that keeps a man at home where things are neat and orderly and under his control. But the answers to his deepest questions are not to be found on television or on his smartphone. Out there on the burning desert sands, lost in a trackless waste, Moses received his life's mission and purpose. If a man is ever to find out who he is and what he's here for, he has got to take that journey for himself. He has got to get his heart back.

....

Dear Heavenly Father, today I choose to turn my face toward you to discover who I am.

What places in your heart are crying out for healing?

_____

_____

_____

What do you long for Jesus to do for you?

_____

_____

_____

Where have I been looking to discover my identity?

_____

_____

_____

Into what are you calling me?

_____

_____

_____

_____

For we are God's handiwork.

EPHESIANS 2:10

I know I am not alone in this nagging sense of failing to measure up, a feeling of not being good enough as *a woman*. Every woman I've ever met feels it—something deeper than just the sense of failing at what she does. An underlying, gut feeling of failing at who she is. *I am not enough*, and *I am too much* at the same time. Not pretty enough, not thin enough, not kind enough, not gracious enough, not disciplined enough. But too emotional, too needy, too sensitive, too strong, too opinionated, too messy. The result is shame, the universal companion of women. It haunts us, nipping at our heels, feeding on our deepest fear that we will end up abandoned and alone. After all, if we were better women—whatever *that* means—life wouldn't be so hard. Right? We wouldn't have so many struggles; there would be less sorrow in our hearts. Why do our days seem so unimportant, filled not with romance and adventure but with duties and demands? We feel unseen, even by those who are closest to us. We feel *unsought*—that no one has the passion or the courage to pursue us, to get past our messiness to find the woman deep inside. And we feel uncertain—uncertain what it even means to be a woman; uncertain what it truly means to be feminine; uncertain if we are or ever will be. Aware of our deep failings, we pour contempt on our own hearts for wanting more. Oh, we long for intimacy and for adventure; we long to be the Beauty of some great story. But the desires set deep in our hearts seem like a luxury, granted only to those women who get their acts together.

....

Lord, I confess that I fear I am not what I should be. Show me how you see me as a woman.

When I became a man, I put the ways of childhood behind me.
1 CORINTHIANS 13:11

ociety at large can't make up its mind about men. "Where are all the real men?" is regular fare for new books. How can a man know he is one when his highest aim is minding his manners? Christianity, as it currently exists, has done damage to masculinity. I think most men in the church believe that God put them on the earth to be a good boy. The problem with men, we are told, is that they don't know how to keep their promises, be spiritual leaders, talk to their wives, or raise their children. But, if they try real hard, they can reach the lofty summit of becoming . . . a nice guy. That's what we hold up as models of Christian maturity: Really Nice Guys. We don't smoke, drink, or swear; that's what makes us men. Now let me ask my male readers: In all your boyhood dreams growing up, did you ever dream of becoming a Nice Guy? (Ladies, was the prince of your dreams dashing . . . or merely nice?) Really now—do I overstate my case? Walk into most churches in America, have a look around, and ask yourself this question: What is a Christian man? Don't listen to what is said; look at what you find there. You'd have to admit a Christian man is . . . bored. A guy in his fifties told me about his journey as a man: "I've pretty much tried for the last twenty years to be a good man as the church defines it." Intrigued, I asked him to say what he thought that was. He paused for a long moment. "Dutiful," he said. "And separated from his heart." A perfect description, I thought.

....

Father, I'm convinced I have been diminished by the world around me.
Teach me what it is to be a man.

What are the ways you fear you're not enough?

_____

_____

_____

What are the ways you fear you're too much?

_____

_____

_____

Who are the iconic "nice guys" you see in our culture?

_____

_____

_____

In your life, who are the men God made them to be?

_____

_____

_____

_____

about HER

> *God created mankind in his own image . . .*
> *male and female he created them.*
>
> GENESIS 1:27

We have missed the *heart* of a woman. And that is not a wise thing to do, for as the Scriptures tell us, the heart is central. "Above all else, guard your heart, for everything you do flows from it" (Proverbs 4:23). Above all else. Why? Because God knows that our heart is core to who we are. It is the source of all our creativity, our courage, and our convictions. It is the fountainhead of our faith, our hope, and of course, our love. This "wellspring of life" within us is the very essence of our existence, the center of our being. Your heart as a woman is the most important thing about you. God created you *as a woman*. Whatever it means to bear God's image, you do so *as a woman*. Your feminine heart has been created with the greatest of all possible dignities—as a reflection of God's own heart. You are a woman to your soul, to the very core of your being. And so the journey to discover what God meant when he created woman in his image—when he created *you* as his woman—that journey begins with your heart. Another way of saying this is that the journey begins with *desire*. The desires that God has placed into our hearts are clues as to who we really are and the role we are meant to play. Many of us have come to despise our desires or at least try to bury them. But the desires of our heart are precisely where we bear the image of God. We long for certain things because *he* does!

· ·

Father, because you created me as a woman, strengthen the core of me that you designed to be feminine.

The LORD is a warrior; the LORD is his name.

EXODUS 15:3

here's a photo on my wall of a little boy about five years old, with an impish grin. The color is fading, but the image is timeless. It's Christmas morning 1964, and I've just opened what may have been the best present ever—a set of two pearl-handled six-shooters, complete with black leather holsters, a red cowboy shirt with two wild mustangs embroidered on either breast, shiny black boots, red bandanna, and straw hat. I donned the outfit and didn't take it off for weeks because it wasn't a costume; it was an identity. Capes and swords, camouflage, bandannas, and six-shooters, all the superhero outfits—these are the uniforms of boyhood. Little boys want to know they are powerful, they are dangerous, they are someone to be reckoned with. How many parents have tried in vain to prevent little Timmy from playing with guns? If you do not supply a boy with weapons, he will make them from whatever materials are at hand. My boys would chew their graham crackers into the shape of handguns at the breakfast table. Every stick or fallen branch was a spear, or better, a bazooka. Despite what many modern educators would say, this is not a psychological disturbance brought on by violent television or chemical imbalance. Healthy aggression is part of the masculine design; we are hardwired for it. If we believe that man is made in the image of God, then we would do well to remember that "the LORD is a warrior; the LORD is his name" (Exodus 15:3). God is a warrior; man is a warrior.

....

Father, because I am hardwired for healthy aggression, make me the warrior you designed me to be.

What are the ways that you have rejected your femininity?

_____

_____

_____

How is God inviting you to recapture your essence as a woman?

_____

_____

_____

Was healthy masculinity encouraged in the home in which you were raised?

_____

_____

_____

How have you embraced your inner warrior, until now?

_____

_____

_____

My beloved is mine and I am his.

SONG OF SONGS 2:16

hen John and I began to "date," I had just come out of a three-year relationship that left me wounded, defensive, and gun-shy. John and I had been friends for many years, but we never seemed to connect in the romance department. I would like him, and he would want to remain "just friends." He would feel more for me, and I would not for him. You get the picture. Until one autumn after he had become a Christian, and I was desperately seeking, our spiritual journeys, and the desires of our hearts, finally met. John wrote me letters, lots of letters. Each one filled with his love for God and his passion for me, his desire for me. He spent hours carving a beautiful heart out of manzanita wood, then attached it to a delicate chain and surprised me with it. (I still cherish the necklace.) I came out to my car after my waitressing shift ended to find his poetry underneath my windshield. Verses written for me, to me! He loved me. He saw me and knew me and pursued me. I loved being romanced. When we are young, we want to be precious to someone—especially our dad. As we grow older, the desire matures into a longing to be pursued, desired, wanted as a woman. "Why am I so embarrassed by the depth of my desire for this?" asked a young friend just the other day. We were talking about her life as a single woman, and how she loves her work but would also like to be married. "I don't want to hang my life on it, but still, I yearn." Of course. You're a woman. You are made for relationship.

....

Lover of my soul, thank you for the reminder that I am made to be pursued, desired, and wanted.

> *Fight for your families, your sons and your*
> *daughters, your wives and your homes.*
>
> NEHEMIAH 4:14

There is nothing so inspiring to a man as a beautiful woman. She'll make you want to charge the castle, slay the giant, leap across the parapets. During a Little League game, my son Samuel was so inspired. He liked baseball, but most boys starting out aren't sure they really have it in them to be a great player. Sam was our firstborn, and like so many firstborns he was cautious. He always let a few pitches go by before he took a swing, and when he did, it was never a full swing; every one of his hits up until that point were in the infield. Anyway, just as Sam stepped up to bat this one afternoon, his friend from down the street, a cute little blonde girl, showed up along the first-base line. Standing up on tiptoe she yelled out his name and waved to Sam. Pretending he didn't notice her, he broadened his stance, gripped the bat a little tighter, looked at the pitcher with something fierce in his eye. First one over the plate he knocked into center field. A man wants to be the hero to the beauty. Young men going off to war carry a photo of their sweetheart in their wallet. Men who fly combat missions will paint a beauty on the side of their aircraft; the crews of the WWII B-17 bomber gave those flying fortresses names like Me and My Gal or the Memphis Belle. What would Robin Hood or King Arthur be without the woman they love? Lonely men fighting lonely battles. Indiana Jones and James Bond just wouldn't be the same without a beauty at their side, and inevitably they must fight for her. You see, it's not just that a man needs a battle to fight; he needs someone to fight for.

· ·

Gracious God of love, awaken my heart to the man in me who wants to
fight for the Beauty!

Have you experienced being pursued and desired?

_____

_____

_____

In what healthy relationship have you seen desire beautifully
expressed?

_____

_____

_____

When have you been a hero to the Beauty?

_____

_____

_____

How might God be inviting you to be the hero today?

_____

_____

_____

about HER

The people who know their God shall stand firm and take action.

DANIEL 11:32 ESV

There is something fierce in the heart of a woman. Simply insult her man, or her best friend, and you'll get a taste of it. Insult her children at your own peril. A woman is a warrior too. But she is meant to be a warrior in a uniquely feminine way. Sometime before the sorrows of life did their best to kill it in us, most young women wanted to be a part of something grand, something important. Before doubt and accusation take hold, most little girls sense that they have a vital role to play; they want to believe there is something in them that is needed and needed desperately. Why do I love remembering the story of canoeing in the dark beauty of the Tetons so much? Because I was needed. *I* was needed. No one else in that canoe could have done what I did. Women love adventures of all sorts. Whether it be the adventure of horses or whitewater rafting, going to a foreign country, performing onstage, climbing mountains, having children, starting a business, or diving ever more deeply into the heart of God, we were made to be a part of a great adventure. An adventure that is *shared*. We do not want the adventure merely for adventure's sake but for what it requires of us *for* others. We don't want to be alone in it; we want to be in it *with* others. Our lives were meant to be lived with others. As echoes of the Trinity, we remember something. We long to be an irreplaceable part of a shared adventure.

....

Wild One, nurture in me a fierce heart and a willingness to pursue adventure.

She is more precious than rubies; nothing you desire can compare with her.

PROVERBS 3:15

ot every woman wants a battle to fight, but every woman yearns to be fought for. Listen to the longing of a woman's heart: she wants to be more than noticed—she wants to be wanted. She wants to be pursued. "I just want to be a priority to someone," a friend in her thirties told me. And her childhood dreams of a knight in shining armor coming to rescue her are not girlish fantasies; they are the core of the feminine heart and the life she knows she was made for. Every woman also wants an adventure to share. To be cherished, pursued, fought for—yes. But also to be strong and a part of the adventure. So many men make the mistake of thinking that the woman is the adventure. But that is where the relationship immediately goes downhill. A woman doesn't want to be the adventure; she wants to be caught up into something greater than herself. And finally, every woman wants to have a beauty to unveil. Most women feel the pressure to be beautiful from very young, but that is not what I speak of. There is also a deep desire to simply and truly be the beauty, and be delighted in. Most little girls will remember playing dress-up, or wedding day, or "twirling skirts," those flowing dresses that were perfect for spinning around in. What she longs for is to capture her daddy's delight. *Do you see me?* asks the heart of every girl. *And are you captivated by what you see?*

....

Warrior God, I long to imitate you. Show me how to fight for the woman I love.

When have you been fierce on behalf of others?　.

_____

_____

_____

What is the adventure for which your heart longs?

_____

_____

_____

How have you "fought for" a woman?

_____

_____

_____

Are you showing and telling your wife that she is captivating?

_____

_____

_____

_____

about HER

You are altogether beautiful.

SONG OF SONGS 4:7

John and I attended a ball at the beautiful, historic Broadmoor Hotel in Colorado Springs. It was a stunning affair. Black tie. Candlelight. Dinner. Dancing. You name it. The courtyard where the hors d'oeuvres were served was filled with fresh flowers, flowing fountains, and the music of a gifted pianist. It was an evening long planned for. For weeks—no, *months* ahead of the affair—I, like every other woman who attended, asked the all-important question: "What will I wear?" The evening turned out to be glorious. The weather was perfect. Every detail attended to and lovely. But the highlight by far was the women. Above the sound of the splashing water from the fountains, even above the music that floated through the air, was the sound of delighted exclamations. "You look beautiful!" "You are gorgeous!" "What an amazing dress!" We were delighting in each other's beauty and enjoying our own. We were playing dress-up for real and *loving it*. These women were normal women, women just like you and me. Women we would run into at the bank or the grocery store. Women whose battles against acne have left their faces marked and their souls scarred. Women whose struggle with their weight has been the bane of their lives. Women who always felt their hair was too thin, too thick, too straight, or too curly. Ordinary women, if there is such a thing. But women who, at least for a few hours this night, took the risk of revealing their beauty. Perhaps better, whose beauty was *unveiled*.

....

Jesus, I confess—and embrace!—that I long to be adored as one who is beautiful.

He trains my hands for battle.

PSALM 18:34

ost of the men I know are trying hard not to become like their fathers. But who does that leave them to follow after? Maybe it would be better to turn our search to that mighty root from which these branches grow. Who is this One we allegedly come from, whose image every man bears? What is he like? In a man's search for his strength, telling him that he's made in the image of God may not sound like a whole lot of encouragement at first. To most men, God is either distant or he is weak— the very thing they'd report of their earthly fathers. What is your image of Jesus as a man? "Isn't he sort of meek and mild?" a friend remarked. "I mean, the pictures I have of him show a gentle guy with children all around. Kind of like Mother Teresa." I'd much rather be told to be like William Wallace. Now—is Jesus more like Mother Teresa or William Wallace? The answer is, it depends. If you're a leper, an outcast, a pariah of society whom no one has ever touched because you are "unclean," then Christ is the incarnation of tender mercy. He reaches out and touches you. On the other hand, if you're a Pharisee, one of those self-appointed doctrine police . . . watch out. On more than one occasion Jesus "picks a fight" with those notorious hypocrites. Christ draws the enemy out, exposes him for what he is, and shames him in front of everyone. The Lord is a gentleman?! Not if you're in the service of his enemy. God has a battle to fight, and the battle is for our freedom.

....

God of battle, instill me with your strength that is quick to fight for what is right.

Has there been someone in your life who affirmed your beauty?

_____

_____

_____

How might you choose to embrace the beauty that is in you?

_____

_____

_____

How have you resisted becoming like your father?

_____

_____

_____

How have you rejected meekness to choose fierce strength?

_____

_____

_____

_____

about HER

He has made everything beautiful in its time.

ECCLESIASTES 3:11

e desire to be captivating in the depths of *who we are*. An external beauty without a depth of character is not true beauty at all. As the Proverb says, "Like a gold ring in a pig's snout is a beautiful woman who shows no discretion" (11:22). Cinderella is beautiful, yes, but she is also good. Her outward beauty would be hollow were it not for the beauty of her heart. That's why we love her. In *The Sound of Music*, the countess has Maria beat in the looks department, and they both know it. But Maria has a rare and beautiful depth of spirit. She has the capacity to love snowflakes on kittens and mean-spirited children. She sees the handiwork of God in music and laughter and climbing trees. Her soul is alive. And we are drawn to her. Ruth may have been a lovely, strong woman, but it is to her unrelenting courage and vulnerability and faith in God that Boaz is drawn. Esther is the most beautiful woman in the land, but it is her bravery and her cunning, good heart that moves the king to spare her people. This isn't about dresses and makeup. The compliment "You are beautiful inside and out" is one that makes our hearts blush. Don't you recognize that a woman yearns to be seen, and to be thought of as captivating? We desire to possess a beauty that is worth pursuing, worth fighting for, a beauty that is core to who we *truly* are. We want beauty that can be seen; beauty that can be felt; beauty that affects others; a beauty all our own to unveil.

....

In the depths of who I am, Lord, I long to be captivating, expressing the beauty that is at my core.

"I have come down to rescue them."

EXODUS 3:8

My buddy Craig and I were after the salmon and giant rainbow trout that live in the icy waters of the Kenai River in Alaska. We were warned about bears, but didn't really take it seriously until we were deep into the woods. Grizzly signs were everywhere—salmon strewn about the trail, their heads bitten off. Piles of droppings the size of small dogs. Huge claw marks on the trees, about head-level. *We're dead,* I thought. *What are we doing out here?* It then occurred to me that after God made all this, he pronounced it good, for heaven's sake. It's his way of letting us know he rather prefers adventure, danger, risk, the element of surprise. This whole creation is unapologetically wild. God loves it that way. Most of us do everything we can to reduce the element of risk in our lives. We wear our seat belts, watch our cholesterol, and practice birth control. Yet this is the world God has made—a world that requires us to live with risk. Because God wants us to live by faith. "Then the Lord intervened" is perhaps the single most common phrase about him in Scripture, in one form or another. Look at the stories he writes. There's the one where the children of Israel are pinned against the Red Sea, no way out, with Pharaoh and his army barreling down on them in murderous fury. Then God shows up. He lets the mob kill Jesus, bury him . . . then he shows up. Do you know why God loves writing such incredible stories? Because he loves to come through. He loves to show us that he has what it takes.

....

God of power, you are the One who rescues! Equip me to be a man who lives by faith.

What actress do you consider to be captivating?

_____

_____

_____

Who is a woman, in your life, you have known to be captivating?

_____

_____

_____

Where, in Scripture, do you see God intervene on behalf of his people?

_____

_____

_____

Where, in your life, has God intervened in a powerful way?

_____

_____

_____

about HER

In the Lord woman is not independent of man,
nor is man independent of woman.

1 CORINTHIANS 11:11

*L*ook at the movies men love—*Braveheart, Gladiator, Top Gun, Saving Private Ryan, Kingdom of Heaven, 1917.* Men are made for battle. (And, ladies, don't you love the heroes of those movies? You may or may not want to fight in a war, but don't you long for a man who will fight for you? To have Hawkeye in *The Last of the Mohicans* look you in the eyes and say, "No matter how long it takes, no matter how far, I will find you"?) Women don't fear a man's strength if he is a good man. In fact, passivity might make a man "safe," but it has done untold damage to women in the long run. It certainly did to Eve. Men also long for adventure. Adventure is a deeply spiritual longing in the heart of every man. Adventure requires something of them, puts them to the test. Though they may fear the test, at the same time they yearn to be tested, to discover that they have what it takes. Finally, every man longs for a Beauty to love. He really does. Where would Robin Hood be without Marian, or King Arthur without Guinevere? Lonely men fighting lonely battles. You see, it's not just that a man needs a battle to fight. He needs someone to fight *for.* There is nothing that inspires a man to courage so much as the woman he loves. This is not to say that a woman is a "helpless creature" who can't live without a man. Men long to offer their strength on behalf of a woman.

···

Lord, I thank you that I am the Beauty for whom you fought and died. Help me to embrace the undeniable beauty I have from you.

> *"You will seek me and find me when you seek me with all your heart."*
>
> JEREMIAH 29:13

ender is a source of great dignity, beauty, honor, and mutual respect. Many good people fear naming the differences between men and women at all, largely because they believe it will usher in discrimination and divisiveness. But this need not be. When we understand just how glorious gender is, how unique and utterly worthy of respect on all sides, I think we can find a better way in our relations. After all, Jesus—the most loving man ever—seemed to think that gender was essential to human understanding: "'Haven't you read,' he replied, 'that at the beginning the Creator "made them male and female"'" (Matthew 19:4). Gender simply must be at the level of the soul, in the deep and everlasting places within us. God doesn't make generic people; he makes something very distinct. In other words, there is a masculine heart and a feminine heart, which in their own ways reflect or portray to the world God's heart. A male lion is awesome to behold, but have you ever seen a lioness? There is also something wild in the heart of a woman, but it is feminine to the core. Often when I am with a woman, I find myself quietly wondering, What is she telling me about God? I know he wants to say something to the world through Eve—what is it? And after years of hearing the heart-cry of women, I am convinced beyond a doubt of this: *God wants to be loved.* He wants to be a priority to someone. From cover to cover, from beginning to end, the cry of God's heart is "Why won't you choose me?"

God who made me in your image, help me to embrace the masculinity that is at the core of who I am.

What story or film of a man's heroic love of a woman most captures your imagination?

_____

_____

_____

When has a man acted heroically on your behalf?

_____

_____

_____

How have you embraced your inherent masculinity?

_____

_____

_____

What do you learn about God from the way he's designed women?

_____

_____

_____

> *The whole earth is full of his glory.*
>
> ISAIAH 6:3

That we even need to explain how beauty is so *absolutely essential* to God only shows how dull we have grown to him, to the world in which we live, and to Eve. Far too many years of our own spiritual lives were lived with barely a nod to the central role that beauty plays in the life of God and in our own lives. We held to the importance of truth and goodness. Had you suggested beauty to us, we might have nodded, but not really understood. Beauty is essential to God. No—that's not putting it strongly enough. Beauty is the essence of God. The first way we know this is through nature, the world God has given us. Scripture says that the created world is filled with the glory of God (Isaiah 6:3). In what way? Primarily through its *beauty*. The earth in summer is brimming with beauty, beauty of such magnificence and variety and unembarrassed lavishness, ripe beauty, lush beauty, beauty given to us with such generosity and abundance it is almost scandalous. Nature is not primarily functional. It is primarily beautiful. Stop for a moment and let that sink in. We're so used to evaluating everything (and everyone) by their usefulness that this thought will take a minute or two to begin to dawn on us. Nature is not primarily functional. It is primarily *beautiful*. Which is to say, beauty is in and of itself a great and glorious good, something we need in large and daily doses (for our God has seen fit to arrange for this). Nature at the height of its glory shouts, *Beauty is essential!* revealing that Beauty is the essence of God. The whole world is full of his glory.

....

Marvelous Creator, forgive me for the ways I neglect your beauty. Open the eyes of my heart to see your glory.

Be strong in the Lord and in his mighty power.

EPHESIANS 6:10

We do not want to teach boys that bullies should never be resisted, and we do not want to teach bullies that they can get away with it! Yes, Scripture teaches the wise use of strength and the power of forgiveness. But you cannot teach a boy to use his strength by stripping him of it. Jesus was able to retaliate, believe me. But he chose not to. And yet we suggest that a boy who is mocked, shamed before his fellows, stripped of all power and dignity should stay in that beaten place because Jesus wants him there? You will emasculate him for life. From that point on all will be passive and fearful. He will grow up never knowing how to stand his ground, never knowing if he is a man indeed. Oh yes, he will be courteous, sweet even, deferential, minding all his manners. It may look moral, it may look like turning the other cheek, but it is merely weakness. You cannot turn a cheek you do not have. Our churches are full of such men.

We must not strip a man of strength and call it sanctification. Yet for many, many men their souls still hang in the balance because no one, no one has ever invited them to be dangerous, to know their own strength, to discover that they have what it takes. Because the assault continues long after the wound has been given. I don't mean to create a wrong impression—a man is not wounded once, but many, many times during his life. Nearly every blow ends up falling in the same place: against his strength. Life takes it away, one vertebra at a time, until in the end he has no spine at all.

··

God of power and might, teach me how to resist the blows of the enemy and stand strong and firm in my manhood.

Where are the places you most readily notice God's beauty?

_____

_____

_____

How will you pause to embrace the beauty God has created?

_____

_____

_____

Was there a voice in your early life that spoke emasculating words to you? How did those words affect you?

_____

_____

_____

How is God calling you into your strength *today*?

_____

_____

_____

A man ... is the image and glory of God; but woman is the glory of man.

1 CORINTHIANS 11:7

She is the crescendo, the final, astonishing work of God. Woman. In one last flourish creation comes to a finish with *Eve*. She is the Master's finishing touch. How we wish this were an illustrated book, and we could show you now a painting or sculpture that captures this, like the stunning Greek sculpture of the goddess Nike of Samothrace, the winged beauty, just alighting on the prow of a great ship, her beautiful form revealed through the thin veils that sweep around her. Eve is breathtaking. Given the way creation unfolds, how it builds to ever higher and higher works of art, can there be any doubt that Eve is the crown of creation? Woman is not an afterthought. Not a nice addition like an ornament on a tree. She is God's final touch, his *pièce de résistance*. She fills a place in the world nothing and no one else can fill. Step to a window, ladies, if you can. Better still, find some place with a view. Look out across the earth and say to yourselves, "The whole, vast world was incomplete without me. Creation reached its finishing touch in me." The story of Eve holds such rich treasures for us to discover. The essence and purpose of a woman is unveiled here in the story of her creation. These profound, eternal, mythic themes are written not just here in the coming of Eve but in the soul of every woman after. Woman is the crown of creation—the most intricate, dazzling creature on earth. She has a crucial role to play, a destiny of her own.

....

Creator God, thank you for making me as the crowning jewel of your creation. Help me embrace the unique role you've given to me.

Fools give full vent to their rage.

PROVERBS 29:11

The real life of the average man seems a universe away from the desires of his heart. There is no battle to fight, unless it's traffic and meetings and hassles and bills. The guys who meet for coffee every Thursday morning down at the local coffee shop and share a few Bible verses with each other—where is their great battle? And the guys who hang out down at the bowling alley, smoking and having a few too many—they're in the exact same place. The swords and castles of their boyhood have long been replaced with pencils and cubicles; the six-shooters and cowboy hats laid aside for minivans and mortgages. Without a great battle in which a man can live and die, the fierce part of his nature goes underground and sort of simmers there in a sullen anger that seems to have no reason. While on a flight to the West Coast during dinnertime, and right in the middle of the meal, the guy in front of me dropped his seat back as far as it could go, with a couple of hard shoves back at me to make sure. I wanted to knock him into first class. Then there was the guy in front of me at a stoplight. It turned green, but he didn't move; I guess he wasn't paying attention. I gave a little toot on my horn to draw his attention to the fact that twenty-plus cars piled up behind us. The guy was out of his car in a flash, yelling threats, ready for a fight. Truth be told, I wanted desperately to meet him there. Men are angry, and we really don't know why.

....

Dear God, I confess that there is anger in me and I offer it to you. Teach me how to notice my anger and honor you in all I do.

How do you feel when you consider that you are the crown of God's creation?

_____

_____

_____

What is one practical way you can embrace your crowning beauty?

_____

_____

_____

When was the last time you got _crazy_ angry?

_____

_____

_____

As you look inside, what is at the root of your anger?

_____

_____

_____

DAY 12

about HER

"It is not good for the man to be alone."

GENESIS 2:18

*G*od wanted to reveal something about himself, so he gave us Eve. When you are with a woman, ask yourself, "What is she telling me about God?" It will open up wonders for you. First, you'll discover that God is relational to his core, that he has a heart for romance. Second, that he longs to share adventures with us—adventures you cannot accomplish without him. And finally, that God has a beauty to unveil. A beauty that is captivating and powerfully redemptive. Eve is created because things were not right without her. Something was not good. "It is not good for the man to be alone" (Genesis 2:18). This just staggers us. The world is young and completely unstained. Adam is yet in his innocence and full of glory. He walks with God. Nothing stands between them. They share something none of us has ever known, only longed for: an unbroken friendship, untouched by sin. Yet something is not good? Something is missing? What could it possibly be? Eve. Woman. Femininity. Wow. Talk about significance. "It is not good for the human to be alone, I shall make him a sustainer beside him" (Genesis 2:18 ALTER). How true this is. Whatever else we know about women, we know they are relational creatures to their cores. The vast desire and capacity a woman has for intimate relationships tells us of God's vast desire and capacity for intimate relationships. In fact, this may be the most important thing we ever learn about God—that he yearns for relationship with us.

....

God, thank you for making me relational at my core, and continue to teach me how to love well.

about HIM

hy does God create Adam? What is a man for? If you know what something is designed to do, then you know its purpose in life. A retriever loves the water; a lion loves the hunt; a hawk loves to soar. It's what they're made for. Desire reveals design, and design reveals destiny. In the case of human beings, our design is also revealed by our desires. Let's take adventure. Adam and all his sons after him are given an incredible mission: rule and subdue, be fruitful and multiply. "Here is the entire earth, Adam. Explore it, cultivate it, care for it—it is your kingdom." Talk about an invitation. This is permission to do a heck of a lot more than cross the street. It's a charter to find the equator; it's a commission to build Camelot. Only Eden is a garden at that point; everything else is wild, so far as we know. No river has been charted, no ocean crossed, no mountain climbed. It's a blank page, waiting to be written. Most men think they are simply here on earth to kill time—and it's killing them. But the truth is precisely the opposite. The secret longing of your heart, whether it's to build a boat and sail it, to write a symphony and play it, to plant a field and care for it—those are the things you were made to do. That's what you're here for. Explore, build, conquer. It's going to take risk, and danger, and there's the catch—are we willing to live with the level of risk God invites us to?

....

Dear God, you know the secret longing of my heart. Give me the courage to be and do what you made me to be and do!

What are the five relationships that are most important in your life?

_____

_____

_____

Is there a relationship to which you need to tend to?

_____

_____

_____

What is your sense of the mission, or purpose, of your life?

_____

_____

_____

How are you, or aren't you, living into that God-given purpose?

_____

_____

_____

"I have loved you with an everlasting love."

JEREMIAH 31:3

Can there be any doubt that God wants to be sought after? The first and greatest of all commands is to love him. He wants us to love him. To seek him with all our hearts. A woman longs to be sought after, too, with the whole heart of her pursuer. God longs to be desired. Just as a woman longs to be desired. This is not some weakness or insecurity on the part of a woman, that deep yearning to be desired. Remember the story of Martha and Mary? Mary chose God, and Jesus said that that is what he wanted. "Mary has chosen what is better" (Luke 10:42). Life changes dramatically when romance comes into our lives. Christianity changes dramatically when we discover that it, too, is a great romance. That God yearns to share a life of beauty, intimacy, and adventure with us. This whole world was made for romance—the rivers and the glens, the meadows and beaches. Flowers, music, a kiss. But we have a way of forgetting all that, losing ourselves in work and worry. Eve—God's message to the world in feminine form—invites us to romance. Through her, God makes romance a priority of the universe. So God endows woman with certain qualities that are essential to relationship, qualities that speak of God. She is inviting. She is vulnerable. She is tender. She embodies mercy. She is also fierce and fiercely devoted. Tender and inviting, intimate and alluring, fiercely devoted. Oh yes, our God has a passionate, romantic heart. Just look at Eve.

....

Jesus, I confess I'm distracted like Martha, and yet I long to spend time in your presence, like Mary. Today I prioritize you.

So she took some of the fruit and ate it. Then she gave some to her husband.

GENESIS 3:6 NLT

efore Eve is drawn from Adam's side and leaves that ache that never goes away until he is with her, God gives Adam some instructions on the care of creation, and his role in the unfolding story. "You may freely eat the fruit of every tree in the garden—except the tree of the knowledge of good and evil" (Genesis 2:16–17 NLT). But notice what God doesn't tell Adam. There is no warning or instruction over what is about to occur: the Temptation of Eve. This is just staggering. Notably missing from the dialogue between Adam and God is something like this: "Adam, one more thing. You and Eve are going to be down in the orchard and something dangerous is going to happen. The eternal destiny of the human race hangs on this moment. Now, here's what I want you to do . . ." He doesn't tell him. He doesn't even mention it, so far as we know. Good grief—why not?! Because God believes in Adam. This is what he's designed to do—to come through. Adam doesn't need play-by-play instructions because this is what Adam is created for. It's already there, everything he needs, in his design, in his heart. Needless to say, the story doesn't go well. Adam fails; he fails Eve and the rest of humanity. Where is Adam, while the serpent is tempting Eve? He's standing right there. He won't risk, he won't fight, and he won't rescue Eve. Our first father—the first real man—gave in to paralysis.

....

Mighty God, I confess the ways I have behaved passively. Today I commit myself to fight for what is good.

Are you naturally more like busy Martha or relational Mary?

_____

_____

_____

How will you make time to linger with Jesus this week?

_____

_____

_____

Where have you seen passivity expressed in your life?

_____

_____

_____

This week, where will you fiercely resist passivity?

_____

_____

_____

_____

> *By his wounds you have been healed.*
>
> 1 PETER 2:24

One of my college roommates was a very pretty young woman, but she didn't know it. She was kind and funny, intelligent and bright. She was also timid and afraid. She spent her evenings camped out in front of her television. Wounded, heartbroken in ways I could only guess at, she found solace in sitcoms and snacks. Hiding women are those of us who never speak up. We stay busy at family gatherings and parties we can't avoid. We'd rather go to a movie than out to dinner with a friend. We don't initiate sex with our husbands ever. We dismiss every compliment. We relinquish major decisions to others. Like Eve after she tasted the forbidden fruit, we hide. We hide behind our makeup. We hide behind our humor. We hide with angry silences and punishing withdrawals. We hide our truest selves and offer only what we believe is wanted, what is safe. We act in self-protective ways and refuse to offer what we truly see, believe, and know. We will not risk rejection or looking like a fool. We have spoken in the past and been met with blank stares and mocking guffaws. We will not do it again. We hide because we are afraid. We have been wounded deeply. To hide means to remain safe, to hurt less. And it has never occurred to us that in all our hiding, something precious in us is also squelched, diminished, and refused—something God needs so very, very much for us to bring to the world.

....

God who heals, I have hidden because I have been wounded and I am afraid. I welcome you to restore what has been squandered.

See, the Lion of the tribe of Judah, the Root of David, has triumphed.

REVELATION 5:5

hy would we put a man in a cage? For the same reason we put a lion there. For the same reason we put God there: he's dangerous. To paraphrase Sayers, we've also pared the claws of the Lion of Judah. A man is a dangerous thing. Women don't start wars. Violent crimes aren't for the most part committed by women. Our prisons aren't filled with women. Obviously, something has gone wrong in the masculine soul, and the way we've decided to handle it is to take that dangerous nature away. Our society produces plenty of boys, but very few men. There are two simple reasons: we don't know how to initiate boys into men; and second, we're not sure we really want to. We want to socialize them, to be sure, but away from all that is fierce, and wild, and passionate. In other words, away from masculinity and toward something more feminine. The strength so essential to men is also what makes them heroes. If a neighborhood is safe, it's because of the strength of men. Slavery was stopped by the strength of men, at a terrible price to them and their families. The Nazis were stopped by men. Apartheid wasn't defeated by women. Who gave up their seats on the lifeboats leaving the *Titanic* so that women and children would be saved? And have we forgotten—it was a Man who let himself be nailed to Calvary's cross.

....

Father God, teach me to walk in the way of brave warriors who defend women and fight for justice. Give me the courage of Jesus on Calvary's cross.

In what ways have you "hidden" yourself?

_____

_____

_____

In what area is God inviting you to come out of hiding?

_____

_____

_____

Do you feel more like a boy or a man on the inside?

_____

_____

_____

What courageous step is God inviting you to take?

_____

_____

_____

_____

about HER

"You will seek me and find me when you seek me with all your heart."

JEREMIAH 29:13

O ne of the deepest ways a woman bears the image of God is in her mystery. By "mystery" we don't mean "forever beyond your knowing," but "something to be explored." "It is the glory of God to conceal a matter," says Proverbs, "to search out a matter is the glory of kings" (25:2). God yearns to be known. But he wants to be *sought after* by those who would know him. He says, "You will seek me and find me when you seek me with all your heart" (Jeremiah 29:13). There is dignity here; God does not throw himself at any passerby. If you would know him you must love him; you must seek him with your whole heart. This is crucial to any woman's soul, not to mention her sexuality. "You cannot simply have me. You must seek me, pursue me. I won't let you in unless I know you love me." Is not the Trinity a great mystery? Not something to be solved, but known with ever-deepening pleasure and awe, something to be enjoyed. Just like God, a woman is not a problem to be solved but a vast wonder to be enjoyed. This is so true of her sexuality. Few women can or even want to "just do it." Foreplay is crucial to her heart, the whispering and loving and exploring of each other that culminates in intercourse. That is a picture of what it means to love her soul. She yearns to be known, and that takes time and intimacy. As she is sought after, she reveals more of her beauty. As she unveils her beauty, she draws us to know her more deeply.

....

God, teach me to seek you with my whole heart. I long to know you, just as I long to be known.

You will be called by a new name that the mouth of the LORD will bestow.

ISAIAH 62:2

n the movie *Gladiator*, the hero is a warrior called Maximus. He is the commander of the Roman armies, a general loved by his men and by the aging emperor Marcus Aurelius. The emperor's foul son Commodus learns of his father's plan to make Maximus emperor in his place, but before Marcus can pronounce his successor, Commodus strangles his father. He sentences Maximus to immediate execution and his wife and son to crucifixion and burning. Maximus escapes, but too late to save his family. Captured by slave traders, he is sold as a gladiator. That fate is normally a death sentence, but this is Maximus, a valiant fighter. He more than survives; he becomes a champion. Ultimately, he is taken to Rome to perform in the Colosseum before the emperor Commodus. After a remarkable display of courage and a stunning upset, the emperor comes down into the arena to meet the valiant gladiator, whose identity remains hidden behind his helmet. When he finally reveals himself, he announces, "My name is Maximus Decimus Meridius; Commander of the Armies of the North; General of the Felix Legions; loyal servant to the true emperor, Marcus Aurelius; father to a murdered son; husband to a murdered wife; and I will have my vengeance, in this life or in the next." The man knows who he is, what he's made of. Where does a man go to learn an answer like that—to learn his true name, a name that can never be taken from him? That deep heart knowledge comes only through a process of initiation.

Mighty God, you alone offer my true identity that can never be taken away.

Where do you feel "unknown" by your spouse?

_____

_____

_____

Are you pursuing God the way you long to be pursued?

_____

_____

_____

In what ways do you resemble Maximus?

_____

_____

_____

And in what particular ways do you *fail* to resemble Maximus?

_____

_____

_____

_____

> *"And surely I am with you always."*
>
> MATTHEW 28:20

*E*ve was given to the world as the incarnation of a beautiful, captivating God—a life-offering, lifesaving lover, a relational specialist, full of tender mercy and hope. She brought a strength to the world, but not a striving, sharp-edged strength. She was inviting, alluring, captivating. Is that how you experience the women you know? Is that how people experience you? Why do so few women have anything close to a life of romance? Loneliness and emptiness are far more common themes—so entirely common that most women buried their longings for romance long ago and are now living merely to get through the week. And it's not just romance—why are most of their relationships fraught with hardship? Their friendships, their families, their best friends all seem to have developed a sort of virus that makes them fundamentally unavailable, leaving a woman lonely at the end of the day. Even when relationships are good, it's never enough. Where does this bottomless pit in us come from? Most women do not feel they are playing an irreplaceable role in a great Story. We struggle to know if we matter at all. If we are at home, we feel ashamed we don't have a "real life" in the outside world. If we have a career, we feel as though we are missing out on more important matters like marriage and children. Most women doubt very much that they have any genuine beauty to unveil. It is, in fact, our deepest doubt. There is nothing captivating about me. Certainly not inside me.

....

God, I am often lonely and empty, yet I know I'm made for more. Teach me to embrace that which is captivating about me.

about HIM

Fathers, do not embitter your children, or they will become discouraged.

COLOSSIANS 3:21

My boys and I were rock climbing in a place called Garden of the Gods. The red sandstone spires look like the dorsal fins of some great beast that surfaced from the basement of time. We all love to climb, and our love for it goes beyond the adventure. There's something about facing a wall of rock, accepting its challenge and mastering it, that calls you out, tests, and affirms what you are made of. As my son Sam ascended the mountain, I was offering words of advice and exhortation. He came to another challenging spot, but this time sailed right over it. A few more moves and he would be at the top. "Sam, you're a wild man!" I shouted. He finished the climb, and I began to get Blaine clipped in. As I was coaching his brother up the rock, Sam sort of sidled up to me and in a quiet voice asked, "Dad . . . did you really think I was a wild man up there?" Miss that moment and you'll miss a boy's heart forever. It's not a question—it's the question, the one every boy and man is longing to ask. *Do I have what it takes? Am I powerful?* Until a man knows he's a man, he will forever be trying to prove he is one, while at the same time shrinking from anything that might reveal he is not. Most men live their lives haunted by the question or crippled by the answer they've been given.

....

Father who is good, thank you for confirming that I have what it takes. Teach me to live into what is most true.

When are the times you notice you are most lonely or empty?

_____

_____

_____

How do you choose to "fill" yourself at those times?

_____

_____

_____

Was there a man in your early life who affirmed you? How?

_____

_____

_____

When you listen for God's voice of affirmation, what do you hear?

_____

_____

_____

_____

"Here is . . . my chosen one in whom I delight."

ISAIAH 42:1

A nytime I am meeting other people, I feel nervous. Often I'm not aware of what I'm truly feeling, but I find myself reapplying lipstick in the car on the way. The more nervous I feel, the more lipstick goes on. I clued into this "habit" some time ago when I caught myself putting on another unnecessary layer. What was I doing? *I was afraid.* At least if my makeup looks good, something deep inside me reasoned, maybe I won't be exposed. Found out. Seen. Every woman is haunted by Eve in the core of her being. She knows intuitively that she is not what she was meant to be. We are more keenly aware of our own shortcomings than anyone else. Remembering the glory that was once ours awakens my heart to an ache that has long gone unfulfilled. It's almost too much to hope for, too much to have lost. You see, every child shares a fundamental longing to be loved. But oftentimes, the way this need plays out is very different. Each child born into this broken world is asking one fundamental question. Little boys want to know, *Do I have what it takes?* For girls, the question is, *Am I lovely?* A woman is fueled by her longing to be delighted in, her longing to be beautiful, to be irreplaceable, to be valued, to have her Question answered, "Yes!"

....

God who loves me, I fear I am not what I was meant to be. Awaken my heart and quicken my ear to hear you confirm that you delight in me.

"You are my Son, whom I love; with you I am well pleased."

LUKE 3:22

To understand how a man receives a wound, you must understand the central truth of a boy's journey to manhood: masculinity is bestowed. A boy learns who he is from a man, or the company of men. He cannot learn it any other place. He cannot learn it from other boys, and he cannot learn it from women. The plan from the beginning of time was that his father would lay the foundation for a young boy's heart, and pass on to him that essential knowledge and confidence in his strength. Dad would be the first man in his life, and forever the most important man. Above all, he would answer the question for his son and give him his name. In Scripture, it is the father who gives the blessing and thereby "names" the son. Adam receives his name from God, and the power of naming. He names Eve, and I believe he also names their sons. Abraham names Isaac, and though Isaac's sons, Jacob and Esau, are apparently named by their mother, they desperately crave the blessing that can only come from their father. The Baptist's father names him John, even though the rest of the family disagrees. Even Jesus needed to hear those words of affirmation from his Father. After he is baptized in the Jordan, before the attack on his identity in the wilderness, his Father speaks: "You are my Son, whom I love; with you I am well pleased" (Luke 3:22). In other words, "Jesus, I am deeply proud of you; you have what it takes."

....

Gracious Father, speak to my heart today and affirm, "You are my son, whom I love; with you I am well pleased." I am listening!

Has there been a man in your life who delighted in who you are?

_____

_____

_____

When you tip your face toward God's, searching for his delight, what do you see?

_____

_____

_____

Was there a man in your life who affirmed who you were as a man?

_____

_____

_____

As you tip your ear toward heaven, can you hear God affirming you the way he affirmed Jesus?

_____

_____

Christ redeemed us from the curse.

GALATIANS 3:13

The curse on Adam cannot be limited *only* to actual thorns and thistles. If that were so, then every man who chooses not to be a farmer would escape the curse. No, the meaning is deeper and the implications are for every son of Adam. Man is cursed with *futility* and *failure*. And failure is a man's worst fear. In the same way, the curse for Eve and all her daughters cannot be limited only to babies and marriage, for if that were true, single woman without children would escape the curse. Rather, woman is cursed with loneliness (relational heartache), with the urge to control (especially her man), and with the dominance of men (which is not how things were meant to be—it is the fruit of the Fall). Aren't your deepest worries and heartaches relational—aren't they connected to someone? Even when things are good, is your vast capacity for intimacy ever filled in a lasting way? There is an emptiness in us that we continually try to feed. For men, what is most deeply marred is his strength. He either becomes a passive, weak man—strength surrendered—or he becomes a violent, driven man—strength unglued. When a woman falls from grace, what is most deeply marred is her tender vulnerability, beauty that invites life. She becomes a dominating, controlling woman—or a desolate, needy, mousy woman. Or some odd combination of both, depending on her circumstances.

....

Jesus, in the face of loneliness, the urge to control, and the dominance of men, make me the woman you meant me to be.

For you, God, tested us.

PSALM 66:10

asculinity is an essence that is hard to articulate but that a boy naturally craves. It is something passed between men. My father taught me to fish. We would spend long days together, trying to catch fish. I will never forget his delight in me when I'd hook one. But the fish were never really the important thing. It was the delight, the contact, the masculine presence gladly bestowing itself on me. "Atta boy, Tiger! Bring him in! That's it . . . well done!" Listen to men when they talk warmly of their fathers and you'll hear the same. Despite the details, what is mostly passed along is the masculine blessing. "Fathers and sons in most tribal cultures live in an amused tolerance of each other," wrote Robert Bly in *Iron John: A Book About Men*. "The son has a lot to learn, and so the father and son spend hours trying and failing together to make arrowheads or to repair a spear or track a clever animal. When a father and son do spend long hours together, which some fathers and sons still do, we could say that a substance almost like food passes from the older body to the younger."[1] This is why my boys loved to wrestle with me—why any healthy boy wants the same with his father. They loved the physical contact, to brush against my cheek, to feel the sandpaper of my whiskers, my strength all around them, and to test theirs on me. And it's that testing that is so essential.

....

God of power, I crave masculinity as I crave food and water. Teach me to embrace who you have designed me to be.

Which is most noticeable in your life: loneliness, the urge to control, or the dominance of men?

_____

_____

_____

How will you respond to this affliction?

_____

_____

_____

When you were a boy, was there a safe man in your life on whom you could test your strength?

_____

_____

_____

Is there a healthy man in your life who affirms your masculinity?

_____

_____

_____

Better to dwell in the wilderness,
Than with a contentious and angry woman.

PROVERBS 21:19 NKJV

self-protective way of relating to others is our gut-level response to a dangerous world. Far too many women forfeit their femininity in order to feel safe and in control. Their strength feels more masculine than feminine. There is nothing inviting or alluring, nothing tender or merciful about them. Controlling women are those of us who don't trust anyone else. No one else is allowed to make a decision that is "ours" to make. We room alone when we travel. We plan perfect birthday parties for our children. It might look as though we're simply trying to be a good mom or a good friend, but what we often do is arrange other people's lives. Controlling women tend to be very well rewarded in this fallen world of ours. We are the ones to receive corporate promotions. We are the ones put in charge of our women's ministries. Can-Do, Bottom-Line, Get-It-Done kinds of women. We never consider that our Martha Stewart perfectionism might not be a virtue. That by living a controlling and domineering life, we are really refusing to trust our God. And it has also never dawned on us that something precious in us is squelched, diminished, and refused. Something that God has given us to bring to the world.

God of love, you know the ways I have resorted to self-protection. Help me as I purpose to share with the world that which is precious in me.

"I am the LORD, who heals you."

EXODUS 15:26

D o I have what it takes? Am I a man, Papa?" Unfortunately, a father's negative response to that question shapes a boy's life. The wounds are devastating. This can get unspeakably evil when it involves physical, sexual, or verbal abuse carried on for years. Without some kind of help, many men never recover. One thing about the assault wounds—they are obvious. However, the passive wounds are not; they are pernicious, like a cancer. Because they are subtle, they often go unrecognized and therefore are actually more difficult to heal. Never receiving any sort of blessing from your father is a wound. Never spending time with him, or getting precious little time, is wounding as well. Some fathers give a wound merely by their silence; they are present, yet absent to their sons Every man carries a wound. No matter how good your life may seem, you live in a broken world full of broken people. Your mother and father, no matter how wonderful, couldn't have been perfect. She is a daughter of Eve, and he a son of Adam. There is no crossing through this country without taking a wound. They may come from other sources—a brother, an uncle, a coach, or a stranger—but every wound, whether it's assaultive or passive, delivers with it a message. The message feels final and true, absolutely true, because it is delivered with such force. Our reaction to it shapes our personality in very significant ways.

....

Dear Papa, I turn my face to you, and you alone, as I ask, "Do I have what it takes?" Speak, Lord; your servant is listening.

What are the ways you've practiced self-protection?

_____

_____

_____

What precious part of you is God inviting you to share with the world?

_____

_____

_____

How did a man affirm you in your youth?

_____

_____

_____

Did the man whom you most needed fail to affirm you? If so, how?

_____

_____

_____

about HER

> *He created them male and female and blessed them.*
>
> GENESIS 5:2

*T*he masculine and feminine run throughout all creation. As C. S. Lewis said, "Gender is a reality, and a more fundamental reality than sex."[1] I am very aware of the pain and confusion the gender debate has caused many people. I believe God's heart aches over his sons and daughters, and their search for identity and belovedness. Genesis 1:26–27 tells us: Then God said, "Let us make mankind in our image, in our likeness"… So God created mankind in his own image, in the image of God he created them; male and female he created them.

Male and female he created us. Gender is a source of great dignity, beauty, honor, and mutual respect. Many people now fear naming the differences between men and women at all, because they believe it will cause discrimination and divisiveness. But when we understand just how glorious gender is, how distinct and complementary, how unique and worthy of respect on all sides, we can find a better way in our relations. After all, Jesus—the most loving man ever—seemed to think that gender was essential to human understanding. God doesn't make generic people; he makes something very distinct—a man or a woman. In other words, there is a masculine heart and a feminine heart, which in their own ways reflect or portray God's heart.

....

Jesus, I put my trust in you because you love me. I open myself to you and welcome you to come for my heart.

about HIM

> *One thing I ask . . . to gaze on the beauty of the*
> *LORD and to seek him in his temple.*
>
> PSALM 27:4

God does not merely want an adventure, but an adventure to share. He didn't have to make us, but he wanted to. Though he knows the name of every star and his kingdom spans galaxies, God delights in being a part of our lives. His heart is for relationship, for shared adventure. And yes, God has a beauty to unveil. There's a reason that a man is captivated by a woman. Eve is the crown of creation. In the Genesis narrative, you'll see that each new stage of creation is better than the one before. First, all is formless, empty, and dark. God begins to fashion the raw materials, like an artist working with a rough sketch or a lump of clay. Light and dark, land and sea, earth and sky—it's beginning to take shape. With a word, the whole floral kingdom adorns the earth. Sun, moon, and stars fill the sky. Surely and certainly, his work expresses greater detail and definition. Next come fish and fowl, porpoises and red-tailed hawks. And then animals, all those amazing creatures. Can you hear the crescendo starting to swell, like a great symphony building and surging higher and higher? The reason a woman wants a beauty to unveil, the reason she asks, Do you delight in me? is simply that God does as well. God is captivating beauty. Can there be any doubt that God wants to be worshiped? That he wants to be seen, and for us to be captivated by what we see?

....

Mighty God, your beauty captivates me, and I worship you for who you are and all you've made.

How have you embraced your gender as an essential part of who you are?

_____

_____

_____

How is your feminine heart *different* from the masculine heart?

_____

_____

_____

Where do you most easily recognize God's beauty in what he has made?

_____

_____

_____

How do you respond when you are moved to worship God?

_____

_____

_____

about HER

"My people . . . have dug . . . broken cisterns."

JEREMIAH 2:13

Whether we tend to dominate and control, or withdraw in our desolation, the ache remains. The deep longings in our hearts just won't go away. And so we indulge. We buy ourselves something nice when we aren't feeling appreciated. We "allow" ourselves a treat when we are lonely and our hearts need soothing. We move into a fantasy world to find some water for our thirsty hearts. But none of these really satisfy, and so we try to fill the remaining emptiness with our little indulgences. Brent Curtis calls them our "little affairs of the heart." God calls them "broken cisterns" (Jeremiah 2:13). They are what we give our hearts to instead of giving them to God. We are endlessly creative in our indulgent pursuits, our adulteries of the heart. Certainly, we do not limit ourselves to just one. Take a moment and consider yours. Where do you go instead of to God when the ache of your heart makes itself known? Shopping, gambling, bingeing, purging, drinking, working, cleaning, exercising, watching TV shows, even our negative emotions can become indulgences. When we camp out in self-doubt, condemning thoughts, or even shame because those emotions have become familiar and comfortable, we are faithlessly indulging rather than allowing our deep ache to draw us to God.

....

Lord, I offer to you my bad habits, my little indulgences, my affairs of the heart that I seek for comfort. Let my deep ache draw me to you.

I was afraid because I was naked; so I hid.

GENESIS 3:10

*A*dam knows now that he has blown it, that something has gone wrong within him, that he is no longer what he was meant to be. Adam doesn't just make a bad decision; he gives away something essential to his nature. He is marred now; his strength is fallen and he knows it. Then what happens? Adam hides. You don't need a course in psychology to understand men. We are hiding, every last one of us. Well aware that we, too, are not what we were meant to be, desperately afraid of exposure, terrified of being seen for what we are and are not, we have run off into the bushes. We hide in our office, at the gym, behind the newspaper and mostly behind our personality. Most of what you encounter when you meet a man is a facade, an elaborate fig leaf, a brilliant disguise. A friend shared with me that he is having a recurring nightmare. It involves a murder, and the FBI. The authorities are closing in, and he knows that any moment he'll be caught. The dream always ends just before he is found out. He wakes in a cold sweat. "Any day now, I'll be found out" is a pretty common theme among us guys. Truth be told, most of us are faking our way through life. We pick only those battles we are sure to win, only those adventures we are sure to handle, only those beauties we are sure to rescue.

....

Father God, I fear that I am not what I was meant to be, and so I hide.
Strengthen me to be the man who charges into battle.

What are the "habits" to which you turn for comfort?

_____

_____

_____

How will you give your deep ache to God this week?

_____

_____

_____

How, specifically, do you hide from God?

_____

_____

_____

Is there a battle, or a mission, into which God is inviting you to enter?

_____

_____

_____

about HER

*The older women . . . can urge the younger women
to love their husbands and children.*

TITUS 2:3-4

For many centuries women lived in close fellowship with other women, allowing many occasions for femininity to naturally pass from older women to younger women. Nowadays those opportunities are nearly gone. The way we see ourselves now was shaped early in our lives. We learned what it meant to be feminine while we were very young. Women learn from their mothers what it means to be a woman, and from their fathers the value that a woman has. If a woman is comfortable with her own femininity, her beauty, her strength, then the chances are good that her daughter will be too. From our mothers we are meant to receive many things, but foremost among them are mercy and tenderness. Our mothers are supposed to show us the merciful face of God. In the best of worlds, we are nurtured at their breasts and cradled in their arms. They rock us to sleep and sing us lullabies. Our youngest years are lived within the proximity of their love, and they care for us in all the meanings of the word. When we get hurt, moms kiss us and make it better. Moms are a bit of a mystery to young girls but also belong to a club that many will one day join. So little girls watch and learn. Little girls learn how to live as women by watching their mothers and grandmothers, and by taking in myriad lessons from all the adult women in their lives.

....

*Lord, I have learned how to be a woman, for better or for worse, from the
women in my life. Teach me to be the woman you made me to be.*

I have fought the good fight.

2 TIMOTHY 4:7

The wound is too well aimed and far too consistent to be accidental. It was an attempt to take you out, to cripple or destroy your strength and get you out of the action. Do you know why there's been such an assault? The Enemy fears you. You are dangerous big-time. If you ever really got your heart back, lived from it with courage, you would be a huge problem to him. You would do a lot of damage . . . on the side of good. Remember how valiant and effective God has been in the history of the world? You are a stem of that victorious stalk.

Most men have never been initiated into manhood. They have never had anyone show them how to do it, and especially, how to fight for their heart. The emasculating culture, the passive church, and the failure of so many fathers have left men without direction. But you can get your heart back. However, if you want the wound healed and your strength restored and to find your true name, you're going to have to fight for it. Do those words cause something in you to stir a little? Does another voice rush in, urging caution, maybe wanting to dismiss me altogether? He's being melodramatic. Or, maybe some guys could, but not me. That's part of the battle.

....

Mighty One, I turn to you today to reveal my heart, heal my wound, restore my strength, and speak my true name. I am ready!

When you were a young girl, which women in your life most shaped you?

_____

_____

_____

What did you learn from your mother about what it means to be a woman?

_____

_____

_____

Until now, how have you offered yourself to God to affirm your masculinity and bestow your identity?

_____

_____

_____

What is one practical way you find your identity in God?

_____

_____

He has sent me to bind up the brokenhearted.

ISAIAH 61:1

ou cannot be alive very long without being wounded. Broken hearts cannot long be avoided in this beautiful yet dangerous world we live in. This is not Eden. Not even close. We are not living in the world our souls were made for. Take a deep look into the eyes of anyone, and behind the smile or the fear, you will find pain. And most people are in more pain than even they realize. Henry Wadsworth Longfellow said, "If we could read the secret history of our enemies, we should find in each man's life sorrow and suffering enough to disarm all hostility."[1] Sorrow is not a stranger to any of us, though only a few have learned that it is not our enemy either. Because we are the ones loved by God—the King of kings, Jesus himself—who came to heal the brokenhearted and set the captives free (Isaiah 61:1), we can take a look back. We can take his hand and remember. We must remember so as not to be held prisoner to the wounds and the messages we received growing up. The horror that abusive fathers inflict on their daughters wounds their souls to their very core, and the assault is obvious. It breaks their hearts, ushers in shame and ambivalence and a host of defensive strategies that shut down their feminine hearts. However, the pain that absent fathers inflict on their daughters is damaging as well, just far harder to see.

....

Tender Jesus, I am in pain. I turn to you as the One who binds up the brokenhearted. Heal my wound.

Am I now trying to win the approval of human beings, or of God?
GALATIANS 1:10

Recently, I met a very successful man I'll call Peter. He was hosting me on the East Coast, and when Peter picked me up at the airport he was driving a new Land Rover with all the bells and whistles. The next day we drove around in his BMW 850CSi. Peter lived in the largest house in town and had a vacation home in Portugal. None of this wealth was inherited; he had worked for every dime. I genuinely liked him. Now here's a man, I said to myself. And yet, there was something missing. You'd think a guy like this would be confident, self-assured, centered. And of course, he seemed like that at first. But as we spent time together I found him to be . . . hesitant. He had all the appearances of masculinity, but it didn't feel like it was coming from a true center.

After several hours of conversation, he admitted he was coming to a revelation. "I lost my father earlier this year to cancer. But I did not cry when he died. You see, we were never really close." Ah yes, I knew what was coming next. "All these years, knocking myself out to get ahead—I wasn't even enjoying myself. What was it for? I see now, I was trying to win my father's approval." A long, sad silence. Then Peter said quietly, through tears, "It never worked." Of course not; it never does. No matter how much you make, no matter how far you go in life, that will never heal your wound or tell you who you are. But, oh, how many men buy into this one.

....

Dear Heavenly Father, I have been driven to prove myself to others. Now I turn my face to you, alone, for affirmation and strength.

Where in your life have you endured suffering?

_____

_____

_____

How has God healed your wounds? What wound will you offer
him?

_____

_____

_____

Who is the man you've turned to for approval?

_____

_____

_____

As you close your eyes and listen for God's voice, what is he
saying to you?

_____

_____

_____

about HER

He heals the brokenhearted and binds up their wounds.

PSALM 147:3

The wounds we received as young girls did not come alone. They brought messages with them, messages that struck at the core of our hearts, right in the place of our Question. Our wounds strike at the core of our *femininity*. The damage is made much worse by the horrible things we believe about ourselves as a result. As children, we didn't have the faculties to process and sort through what was happening to us. If we were overwhelmed or belittled or hurt or abused, we believed that somehow it was because of *us*—the problem was with us. Women are always looking for something to work on. Prayer, exercise, financial responsibility, a new hair color. Why do we try so hard? We simply fear that somehow we are not enough. Deep down we fear there is something terribly wrong with us. We can't help but believe that if we were different, if we were *better*— someone funnier, someone smarter, someone else—then we would have been loved as we so longed to be. It must be us. What was your childhood like? Did you know to the core of your being that you were loved, special, worth protecting, and wanted? I pray so. But I know that for many of you, the childhood you wanted to have, the childhood you were meant to have, is a far cry from the childhood you *did* have.

....

God, I turn my ear toward you. I hear you affirming that I am loved, special, worth protecting, and wanted. Lord, I believe; help my unbelief!

I saw that wisdom is better than folly.

ECCLESIASTES 2:13

After years of trying to succeed in the world's eyes, a friend still clings stubbornly to that idea. Sitting in my office, he says to me, "Who's the real stud? The guy making money."

Men take their souls' search for validation in all sorts of directions. Brad is a good man who for so many years has been searching for a sense of significance through belonging. As he said, "Out of my wounds I figured out how to get life: I'll find a group to belong to, do something incredible that others will want, and I'll be somebody." First it was the right gang of kids in school; then it was the wrestling team; years later, it was the right ministry team. It has been a desperate search, by his own admission. And it hasn't gone well. When things didn't work out earlier this year at the ministry he was serving, he knew he had to leave. "My heart has burst and all the wounds and arrows have come pouring out. I have never felt such pain." Where does a man go for a sense of validation? To what he owns? To who pays attention to him? How attractive his wife is? How well he plays sports? The world cheers on the vain search: make a million, run for office, get a promotion, hit a home run . . . be somebody. Can you feel the mockery of it all?

....

God, my soul has sought validation in what the world values. Forgive me, deliver me, and teach me to find my life in you.

What do you do to make yourself seem more valuable or worthy?

_____

_____

_____

Can you hear God's voice affirming that you matter deeply to him?

_____

_____

In what ways have you pursued the world's standards of success?

_____

_____

_____

Can you hear God affirming that you belong, you are wanted, and you are not alone?

_____

_____

about HER

Instead of your shame you will receive a double portion.

ISAIAH 61:7

As a result of the wounds we receive growing up, we come to believe that some part of us, maybe every part of us, is marred. Shame enters in and makes its crippling home deep within our hearts. We avoid eye contact with strangers and friends. We feel that if someone really knew us, they would shake their heads in disgust and run away. Shame makes us believe that we do not measure up—not to the world's standards, the church's standards, or our own standards. Others seem to master their lives, but shame grips our hearts, ever ready to point out our failures and judge our worth. We are lacking. We know we are not all that we long to be, all that God longs for us to be, but instead of coming up for grace-filled air and asking God what he thinks of us, shame keeps us pinned down and gasping. If we were not deemed worthy of love as children, it is incredibly difficult to believe we are worth loving as adults We are afraid of being truly seen, and so we hide our truest selves and offer only what we believe is wanted. We are silent when what we see or know is different from what others are saying, because we think we must be wrong. We refuse to bring the weight of our lives, who God has made us to be, to bear on others out of a fear of being rejected.

....

God, I confess that I have believed I am unworthy, broken, and beyond repair. Speak your true word to my heart. I put my trust in you.

Flee the evil desires of youth and pursue righteousness.

2 TIMOTHY 2:22

I f a man can feel like the hero sexually, well then, he's the hero. Pornography is so seductive because it offers a wounded, famished man literally thousands of beauties willing to give themselves to him? It's unbelievable how many movies center around this lie. Get the beauty, win her, bed her, and you are the man. You're James Bond. You're a stud. Bruce Springsteen even wrote a song where he sung about how every woman has this place inside that's everything a man wants, everything a man needs. It's a deep lie wedded to a deep truth. Eve is a garden of delight (Song of Solomon 4:16). But she's not everything you want, everything you need— not even close. Don't get me wrong. A woman is a captivating creature. More captivating than anything else in all creation, her naked body a portion "of Eternity too great for the eye of man."[1] Femininity can arouse masculinity. All systems alert. But femininity can never bestow masculinity. It's like asking a pearl to give you a buffalo. It's like asking a field of wildflowers to give you a '57 Chevy. They are different substances entirely.

....

God of strength, I thank you for the beauty and worth of my woman, but I turn to you alone to bestow masculinity.

In what ways do you feel like you don't live up to the world's standards, the church's standards, or your own standards?

_____

_____

_____

Why do you believe you are unworthy?

_____

_____

_____

In what moments has your wife aroused your masculinity?

_____

_____

_____

How have you unwisely expected your wife to _bestow_ your masculinity?

_____

_____

_____

Those who hope in the L\ord will renew their strength.

ISAIAH 40:31

Over the years we've come to see that the only thing *more* tragic than the things that have happened to us is what we have done with them. Words were said, painful words. Things were done, awful things. And they shaped us. Something inside of us *shifted*. We embraced the messages of our wounds. We accepted a twisted view of ourselves. And from that we chose a way of relating to our world. A woman who is living out of a broken, wounded heart is a woman who is living a self-protective life. We may not even be aware of it. We also developed ways of trying to get something of the love our hearts cried out for. Despite the best face we put on, the ache is there. As Proverbs says, "Even in laughter the heart may ache" (14:13). Our desperate need for love and affirmation, our thirst for some taste of romance and adventure and beauty, is there. So we turned to boys or to food or to myriad available distractions; we lost ourselves in our work or at church or in some sort of service. All this adds up to the women we are today. Much of what we call our "personalities" is actually the mosaic of our choices for self-protection plus our plan to get the love we were created for. The problem is our plan has nothing to do with God. The wounds we received and the messages they brought formed a sort of unholy alliance with our fallen nature as women. From Eve we received a deep mistrust in the heart of God toward us.

....

Healing God, I have turned to false substitutes to heal and fill me. I turn toward you now to offer what only you can.

> *If anyone, then, knows the good they ought to*
> *do and doesn't do it, it is sin for them.*
>
> JAMES 4:17

A dam falls, and all his sons with him. After that, what do you see as the story unfolds? Violent men, or passive men. Strength gone bad. Cain kills Abel; Lamech threatens to kill everybody else. God finally floods the earth because of the violence of men, but it continues. Sometimes it's physical; most of the time, it's verbal. I know Christian men who say the most awful things to their wives. Or they tear them apart with their silence. I know pastors, warm and friendly guys in the pulpit, who send out blistering emails to their staff. It's cowardice, all of it. The violence, no matter what form, is a cover-up for fear. What about the achievers, the men running hard at life, pressing their way ahead? Most of it is fear-based as well. For years, I was a driven, type-A perfectionist. I demanded a lot of myself and of those who worked for me. All that swaggering and supposed confidence and hard charging came out of fear—the fear that if I did not, I would reveal that I was less than a man. Never let down, never drop your guard, give 150 percent. Achievers are a socially acceptable form of violent men, overdoing it in one way or another. Their casualties tend to be their marriages, their families, and their health. Until a man faces this honestly, and what's really behind it, he'll do great damage.

....

God of power, I confess that I fear being found out and exposed as being
less than a man. Teach me to rest in who you've made me.

In what ways have you tried to get love outside of God?

_____

_____

_____

What have been the results of your attempts to secure love?

_____

_____

_____

In what ways has violence been a cover-up for fear in your life?

_____

_____

_____

What is at risk if you continue in anger or violence?

_____

_____

_____

_____

about HER

"When you pass through the waters, I will be with you."

ISAIAH 43:2

If you listen carefully to any woman's story, you will hear a theme: the assault on her heart. It might be obvious as in the stories of physical, verbal, or sexual abuse. Or it might be more subtle, the indifference of a world that cares nothing for her but uses her until she is drained. Either way, the wounds continue to come long after we've grown up, but they all seem to speak the same message. Our Question is answered again and again throughout our lives, the message driven home into our hearts. As women we tend to feel that it must be us That's the effect of our early wounds. "Something is fundamentally wrong with me." So many women feel that way. We also feel we are essentially alone. That somehow the two are related. We believe we are alone because we are not the women we should be. We don't feel worthy of pursuit. So we hang a Do Not Disturb sign on our personalities, send a "back off" message to the world. Or we desperately seek pursuit, losing all self-respect in an emotional and physical promiscuity. We don't feel we are irreplaceable, so we try to make ourselves useful. We don't believe we are beautiful, so we work hard to be outwardly beautiful, *or* we "let ourselves go" and hide behind a persona that has no allure. We try so hard, and in so many ways, to protect our hearts from further pain.

....

Jesus, I have endured an assault on my heart that has convinced me I am problematic. Speak your true word that affirms who I really am.

You knit me together in my mother's womb.

PSALM 139:13

Years ago, at a point in my own journey when I felt more lost than ever, I heard a talk given by Gordon Dalbey, who had just written *Healing the Masculine Soul*. He raised the idea that despite a man's past and the failures of his own father to initiate him, God could take him on that journey and provide what was missing. A hope rose within me, but I dismissed it with the cynicism I'd learned to use. Later, in the early morning, during my morning time, I looked out the window toward the east to watch the sun rise. I heard Jesus whisper a question to me: "Will you let me initiate you?" Before my mind ever had a chance to process and doubt the whole exchange, my heart leaped up and said yes. "Who can give a man this, his own name?" George MacDonald asked. "God alone. For no one but God sees what the man is."[1] He reflects upon the white stone that Revelation includes among the rewards God will give to those who overcome. On that white stone there is a new name. It is not the name the world gave to us, certainly not the one delivered with the wound. The new name is really not new at all when you understand that it is your true name, the one that belongs to you, "that being whom he had in his thought when he began to make the child, and whom he kept in his thought through the long process of creation"[2] and redemption.

....

God who heals, I long to be initiated by you. Speak my new name, and help me see what you see.

When was the moment in which your heart was assaulted?

_____

_____

_____

How have you responded to that assault?

_____

_____

_____

What was the name the world gave you?

_____

_____

_____

As you listen for God's voice, what name does he call you?

_____

_____

_____

_____

> *How you have fallen from heaven, morning star.*
>
> ISAIAH 14:12

Turn your attention again to the events that took place in the Garden of Eden. Who does the Evil One go after? Who does Satan single out for his move against the human race? He could have chosen Adam . . . but he didn't. Satan went after Eve. Have you ever wondered why? It might have been that he, like any predator, chose what he believed to be the weaker of the two. But we believe there are other reasons. You may know that Satan was first named Lucifer, or Son of the Morning. It infers a glory, a brightness or radiance unique to him. Lucifer was gorgeous. He was breathtaking. And it was his ruin. Pride entered Lucifer's heart. He craved for himself the worship that was being given to God. He didn't merely want to play a noble role in the Story; he wanted the Story to be about *him*. He wanted the attention, the adoration for himself. Satan fell *because* of his beauty. Now his heart for revenge is to assault beauty. He destroys it in the natural world wherever he can. Oil spills, fires, pollution. He wreaks destruction on the glory of God in the earth. But *most* especially, he hates Eve. Because she is captivating, uniquely glorious—and he cannot be. She is the incarnation of the Beauty of God. More than anything else in all creation, she embodies the glory of God. She allures the world to God.

God, I feel Satan's envy and hatred. Deliver me. Teach me to rest in the beauty you have bestowed on my soul.

Teach me your way, Lord.

PSALM 86:11

*E*ven if your father did his job, he can only take you partway. There comes a time when you have to leave all that is familiar, and go on into the unknown with God. Saul was a guy who thought he understood the story and liked the part he had written for himself. After the Damascus Road, rather than heading back into all the old and familiar ways, he is led for three years to learn directly from God. Jesus shows us that initiation can happen even when we've lost our father or grandfather. He's the carpenter's son. But when we meet the young man Jesus, Joseph is out of the picture. Jesus has a new teacher—his true Father—and it is from him he must learn who he really is and what he's really made of. Initiation involves a journey and a series of tests, through which we discover our real name and our true place in the story. Most of us are asking, "God, why did you let this happen to me?" Or, "God, why won't you just . . ." But to enter into a journey of initiation with God requires a new set of questions:

+ What are you trying to teach me here?
+ What is it you want me to see?
+ What are you asking me to let go of?

In truth, God has been trying to initiate you for a long time.

....

God who redeems, I turn toward your face to discover who I am. I am listening for what you will teach my heart.

Where has Satan caused destruction in your life?

_____

_____

_____

Where do you need God's deliverance?

_____

_____

_____

When you think of a tricky issue in your life, what could God be trying to teach you?

_____

_____

_____

Is there anything there that you need to release?

_____

_____

_____

_____

about HER

Turn to me and be gracious to me, for I am lonely and afflicted.

PSALM 25:16

To do any sort of justice to a book for women would require me (John) to go deeper, listen even more carefully, study, delve into the mystery (okay, mess) of a woman's soul. Part of me didn't want to go there. Pull back. Withdraw. I was keenly aware of this going on inside me, and I felt like a jerk. But I also knew enough about myself and about the battle for a woman's heart that I needed to explore this ambivalence. What is this thing in me—and in most men—that doesn't want to go deep into a woman's world? "You are too much. It's too much work. Men are simpler. Easier." And isn't that the message you've lived with all your life as a woman? "You're too much, and not enough. You're just not worth the effort." Now, part of a man's fundamental reluctance to truly dive into the world of a woman comes from a man's deepest fear: failure. He fears that having delved into his woman's world, he won't have what it takes to help her there. That is his sin. That is his cowardice. And because of her shame, most of the time a man gets away with it. Most marriages reach this sort of unspoken settlement. "I'm not coming any closer. This is as far as I'm willing to go. But I won't leave, and that ought to make you happy." And so there is this sort of détente, a cordial agreement to live only so close. The effect is that most women feel alone.

....

Lord Jesus, you know the ways in which I feel alone. Give my husband courage to come near, even as I draw near to you.

For I am poor and needy, and my heart is wounded within me.

PSALM 109:22

or most of us, our wounds are an immense source of shame. A man's not supposed to get hurt; he's certainly not supposed to let it really matter. And so most men minimize their wounds. King David (a guy who was hardly a pushover) didn't act like that at all. "I am poor and needy," he confessed openly, "and my heart is wounded within me" (Psalm 109:22). Or perhaps men will admit it happened, but deny it was a wound because they deserved it. After many months of counseling, I asked Dave a simple question: "What would it take to convince you that you are a man?" "Nothing," he said. "Nothing can convince me." We sat in silence as tears ran down my cheeks. He had embraced the wound and owned its message as final. There was no sign of emotion at all. I went home and wept—for Dave, and for so many other men I know, and for myself because I realized that I, too, had embraced my wound. The only thing more tragic than the tragedy that happens to us is the way we handle it. God is fiercely committed to you, to the restoration and release of your masculine heart. But a wound that goes unacknowledged and unwept is a wound that cannot heal. A wound you've embraced is a wound that cannot heal. A wound you think you deserved is a wound that cannot heal.

....

God, give me the courage to acknowledge my wound so that I might heal. I trust you to restore me and release my masculine heart.

Has a man in your life communicated that you are too much or not enough? How did this affect your heart?

_____

_____

_____

What does God say about who you are?

_____

_____

_____

Have you ever been physically injured and ignored it? What happened?

_____

_____

_____

Have you ever quietly believed you *deserved* the wounds you've endured?

_____

_____

> *For Zion's sake I will not keep silent.*
>
> ISAIAH 62:1

To every woman, from the day of her birth Satan has whispered, "You are alone," or "When they see who you really are, you will be alone," or "No one will ever truly come for you." Take a moment. Quiet your heart and ask yourself, "Is this a message I have believed, feared, lived with?" Not only do most women fear they will ultimately be abandoned by the men in their lives, they fear it from other women as well—that they will be abandoned by their friends and left alone. It's time to reveal this pervasive threat, this crippling fear, this terrible lie. The Enemy bears a special hatred for Eve. If you believe he has any role in the history of this world, you cannot help but see it. The Evil One had a hand in all that has happened to you. If he didn't arrange for the assault directly—and certainly human sin has a large enough role to play—then he made sure he drove the message of the wounds home into your heart. He is the one who has dogged your heels with shame and self-doubt and accusation. He is the one who offers the false comforters to you to deepen your bondage. He is the one who has done these things to prevent your restoration. For that is what he fears. He fears who you are, what you are, what you might become. He fears your beauty and your life-giving heart.

....

Father of love, I have listened to the Enemy's lies. I have feared being abandoned. Do not stay silent. Deliver me from this crippling lie and strengthen me to stand on your truth.

But the Lord God called to the man, "Where are you?"

GENESIS 3:9

*G*od thwarts us to save us. We think it will destroy us, but the opposite is true—we must be saved from what will destroy us. If we desire to walk with him in our journey of masculine initiation, we must walk away from the false self—set it down, give it up willingly. It feels crazy; it feels immensely vulnerable. We simply accept the invitation to leave all that we've relied on and venture out with God. We can choose to do it ourselves, or we can wait for God to bring it all down. If you have no clue as to what your false self may be, then a starting point would be to ask those you live with and work with, "What is my effect on you? What am I like to live with (or work with)? What don't you feel free to bring up with me?" If you never say a word in a meeting because you fear you might say something stupid, it's time to speak up. If all you ever do is dominate a meeting because your sense of worth comes from being in charge, then you need to shut up for a while. If you've turned to sports because you feel best about yourself there, then maybe it's time to take a break and be with your family. In other words, you face your fears head-on. Drop the fig leaf; come out from hiding. For how long? Long enough to raise the deeper issues and let the wound surface from beneath it all.

....

Lord of life, I admit that I have embraced my false self. Today, though, I relinquish it willingly as I come out of hiding.

Have you feared that when others find out who you really are, they will reject you? When?

_____

_____

_____

What Scripture verse helps you claim what is truer?

_____

_____

_____

What are the ways you have hidden behind a false self?

_____

_____

_____

What is one practical way you can reject that false self?

_____

_____

_____

_____

"I will block her path with thornbushes."

HOSEA 2:6

hy did God curse Eve with loneliness and heartache, an emptiness that nothing would be able to fill? Wasn't her life going to be hard enough out there in the world, banished from the Garden that was her home, never able to return? It seems unkind. But he did it to *save* her. For as we all know personally, something in Eve's heart shifted at the Fall. Something sent its roots down deep into her soul and ours—that mistrust of God's heart, that resolution to find life on our own terms. So God has to thwart her. In love, he has to block her attempts until, wounded and aching, she turns to him for her rescue. Jesus has to thwart us too—thwart our self-redemptive plans, our controlling and our hiding, thwart the ways we are seeking to fill the ache within us. Otherwise, we would never fully turn to him for our rescue. Oh, we might turn to him for our salvation, for a ticket to heaven when we die. We might turn to him even in the form of Christian service, regular church attendance, a moral life. But inside, our hearts remain broken and captive and far from the One who can help us. And so you will see the gentle, firm hand of God in a woman's life hemming her in. Wherever it is we have sought life apart from him, he disrupts our plans, our "way of life" that is not life at all.

....

Lord, I have sought my life apart from you. Forgive me. And I welcome the thornbushes, the obstacles, that are steering me back toward your heart.

And Adam was not the one deceived; it was the woman
who was deceived and became a sinner.

1 TIMOTHY 2:14

There was a time when Adam drank deeply from the source of all Love. He—our first father and archetype—lived in an unbroken communion with the most captivating, beautiful, and intoxicating Source of life in the universe. Adam had God. True, it was not good for man to be alone, and God in his humility gave us Eve, allowed us to need her as well. But something happened at the Fall; something shifted. Eve took the place of God in a man's life. Adam was not deceived by the serpent. Paul made it clear in 1 Timothy 2:14—Adam did not fall because he was deceived. His sin was different; in some ways, it was more serious in that he did it with open eyes. There was a moment in Eden when Eve was fallen and Adam was not; she had eaten, but he still had a choice. I believe something took place in his heart: he had lost his soul mate, the most vital companion Adam chose Eve over God. As you get closer to your wound, the longing for the ache to go away and the pull toward other comforters can seem overwhelming. I've watched it in many men. I know it in myself. But if this is the water you are truly thirsty for, then why do you remain thirsty after you've had a drink? It's the wrong well. For only in God will we find the healing of our wound.

....

God of life, I confess that I have drunk from the wrong well, seeking my life in that which is not you. Draw me to your heart and heal my wound.

How have you sought to build a secure life outside of God?

_____

_____

_____

What are the obstacles you're facing as a result? What obstacles
has God already helped you overcome?

_____

_____

_____

Are there ways you've chosen a woman over God?

_____

_____

_____

What is one practical way, this week, that you can drink from
the well that truly satisfies?

_____

_____

_____

about HER

> *"Behold, I stand at the door and knock. If anyone hears*
> *My voice and opens the door, I will come in."*
>
> REVELATION 3:20 NKJV

*J*esus does not force himself upon us. He knocks and waits for us to ask him in. There is an initial step, which we call salvation. We hear Christ knocking and we open our hearts to him as Savior. But the principle of this "knocking and waiting for permission to come in" remains true well into our Christian life. We all pretty much handle our brokenness in the same way—we mishandle it. It hurts too much to go there. So we shut the door to that room in our hearts, and we throw away the key. But that does not bring healing. Not at all. It might bring relief—for a while. But never healing. The best thing we can do is let Jesus come in; open the door and invite him in to find us in those hurting places. It might come as a surprise that Christ asks our permission to come in and heal, but he is kind, and the door is shut from the inside, and healing never comes against our will. Give him permission. Give him access to your broken heart. Ask him to come to *these* places. Yes, Jesus, yes. I do invite you in. Come to my heart in these shattered places. Come to me, my Savior. I open this door of my heart. I give you permission to heal my wounds. Come to me here. Come for me here.

....

Sweet Jesus, I hear you knocking, and I welcome you in! I open the shattered places in my heart and give you permission to heal my wounds.

"Apart from me you can do nothing."

JOHN 15:5

*L*et me tell you of my favorite time when our boys were young. It came late in the evening, at bedtime, after the boys had brushed their teeth and we said our family prayers. As I was tucking them in, one of them would ask, "Dad, can we snuggle tonight?" Snuggle time was when I'd cuddle up next to them on a bed that really wasn't big enough for both of us, and there in the dark we'd talk. Usually we'd start laughing and then we'd have to whisper because the others would ask us to "keep it down in there." Sometimes it broke into tickling, other times it was a chance for them to ask some serious questions about life. But whatever happened, what mattered most was what was going on beneath all that: intimacy, closeness, connection. Yes, my boys wanted me to guide them into adventure, and they loved to test their strength against mine. But all of that took place in the context of an intimate bond of love that is far deeper than words can express. What they wanted more than anything, what I loved to offer them more than anything, was soul-to-soul oneness. From the very beginning, ours was meant to be a desperately dependent existence. Jesus said, "Apart from me you can do nothing" (John 15:5). We are made to depend on God; we are made for union with him, and nothing about us works right without it.

. . . .

Strong Father, I seek my identity in you. You are the source of my life, and I depend on you. Nourish me with your life.

What is the wound inside that you've not allowed Jesus to touch?

_____

_____

_____

What is one practical way, this week, that you will spend time with Jesus in that place?

_____

_____

_____

Was there a man in your early life with whom you could snuggle or wrestle?

_____

_____

_____

How are you being nourished as a branch attached to the trunk?

_____

_____

Put my tears into Your bottle.

PSALM 56:8 NKJV

Part of the reason women are so tired is because we are spending so much energy trying to "keep it together." So much energy devoted to suppressing the pain and keeping a good appearance. Part of this is driven by fear that the pain will overwhelm us. That we will be consumed by our sorrow. It's an understandable fear—but it is no more true than the fear we had of the dark as children. Grief, dear sisters, is good. Grief helps to heal our hearts. Jesus himself was a "Man of sorrows and acquainted with grief" (Isaiah 53:3 NKJV). Let the tears come. It is the only kind thing to do for your woundedness. Allow yourself to feel again. And feel you will—many things. Anger. Remorse and regret for so many lost years. Fear. Jesus can handle the fear as well. In fact, there is no emotion you can bring up that Jesus can't handle. (The psalms are a raging sea of emotions.) Let it all out. Grief is a form of validation; it says the wound *mattered*. You mattered. That's not the way life was supposed to go. There are unwept tears down in there—the tears of a little girl who is lost and frightened. The tears of a teenage girl who's been rejected and has no place to turn. The tears of a woman whose life has been hard and lonely and nothing close to her dreams. Let the tears come.

....

Jesus, I offer you the unwept tears of this girl who is lost and frightened. Rejected. Challenged. Lonely. I offer my grief to you, with confidence that you care.

> *"The Son can do nothing by himself; he can do*
> *only what he sees his Father doing."*
>
> JOHN 5:19

We come to believe deep in our hearts that needing anyone for anything is a sort of weakness, a handicap. This is why a man never stops to ask for directions. I am notorious for this. I know how to get there; I'll find my own way. Only when I am completely lost will I pull over and get some help, and I'll feel like a wimp for doing it. Jesus knew nothing of that. The Man who never flinched to take on hypocrites and get in their face, the Master of wind and sea, lived in a desperate dependence on his Father. "I assure you, the Son can do nothing by himself. He does only what he sees the Father doing"; "I live by the power of the living Father who sent me." This isn't a source of embarrassment to Christ; quite the opposite. He's happy to tell anyone who will listen, "The Father and I are one" (John 5:19; 6:57; 10:30). Why is this important? Because so many men I know live with a deep misunderstanding of Christianity. They look at it as a "second chance" to get their act together. They've been forgiven; now they see it as their job to get with the program. They're trying to finish the marathon with a broken leg. But remember that masculinity is an essence that is passed from father to son. That is a picture of a deeper reality. The true essence of strength is passed to us from God through our union with him.

....

Father God, I hate to admit my need. I'd rather be independent! Make me more like Jesus, who didn't make a move without you.

Do you find it easy or difficult to cry? Why is that?

_____

_____

_____

What is the area of your life that you most need to grieve? How
has grieving helped you in the past?

_____

_____

_____

How have you "played through the pain" in your life?

_____

_____

_____

Where, in Jesus' life, do you witness him depending on his
Father? How can you apply this to your own life?

_____

_____

_____

Forgive as the Lord forgave you.

COLOSSIANS 3:13

*W*e must forgive those who hurt us. The reason is simple: bitterness and unforgiveness set their hooks deep in our hearts; they are chains that hold us captive to the wounds and the messages of those wounds. Until you forgive, you remain their prisoner. Paul warns us that unforgiveness and bitterness can wreck our lives and the lives of others (Ephesians 4:31; Hebrews 12:15). We have to let it all go. Forgiveness is a choice. It is not a feeling. It is an act of the will. "Don't wait to forgive until you feel like forgiving," wrote Neil Anderson. "You will never get there. Feelings take time to heal after the choice to forgive is made." We allow God to bring the hurt up from our past, for "if your forgiveness doesn't visit the emotional core of your life, it will be incomplete," said Anderson.[1] We acknowledge that it hurt, and we choose to extend forgiveness. Forgiveness says, "It was wrong. Very wrong. It hurt me deeply. And I release you. I give you to God. I will not be your captive here any longer." It might help to remember that those who hurt you were also deeply wounded themselves. This doesn't absolve them of the choices they made, the things they did. It just helps us to let them go—to realize that they were shattered souls themselves, used by our true Enemy in his war against femininity.

Lord, I confess I have withheld forgiveness—for all the wrong reasons. Give me the courage to notice my hurt, agree that it matters, and still forgive.

about HIM

He drove out the spirits with a word and healed all the sick.

MATTHEW 8:16

*O*f you wanted to learn how to heal the blind and you thought that following Christ around and watching how he did it would make things clear, you'd wind up pretty frustrated. He never does it the same way twice. There are no formulas with God. The way in which God heals our wound is a deeply personal process. He is a person and he insists on working personally. For some, it comes in a moment of divine touch. For others, it takes place over time and through the help of another, maybe several others. So much healing took place in my life simply through my friendship with Brent. We were business partners, but far more than that, we were friends. We spent hours together fly-fishing, backpacking, hanging out in pubs. Just spending time with a man I truly respected, a real man who loved and respected me—nothing heals quite like that. Even though I feared that he'd see through my disguise any day and drop me, he didn't, and what happened instead was validation. My heart knew that if a man I consider a man thinks I'm one too, maybe I am one after all. Remember—masculinity is bestowed by masculinity. But there have been other significant ways in which God has worked—times of healing prayer, times of grieving the wound and forgiving my father. Most of all, times of deep communion with God. The point is this: healing never happens outside of intimacy with Christ. The healing of our wound flows out of our union with him.

....

Jesus, I see you healing in myriad ways, and I trust that you are healing my wounds as I draw near to you.

Who wounded you that you have not yet forgiven?

_____

_____

_____

What practical step toward forgiveness will you choose to take
this week?

_____

_____

_____

What man has affirmed your masculinity?

_____

_____

_____

How will you pursue intimacy with Christ so that he might heal
your wound?

_____

_____

_____

See what great love the Father has lavished on us.

1 JOHN 3:1

I have heard many times that what we first believe about God the Father comes from what we know of and have experienced from our earthly dads. When I first heard this, I thought that the idea itself was ludicrous. Of course, my own dad was not God. Everybody knew that. But later, as I heard other women speak of God the Father, I often heard in their voices a softness, a tenderness, perhaps even a childlikeness that was foreign to me. When I began to hear others praying to "Daddy" or "Papa," I knew they were speaking to Someone I did not know. I had never called my own father "Daddy." Many of us grew up in homes where the correct term for Dad was "Sir." Intimacy with and dependence on a father who was rarely home—and emotionally absent when he was—was impossible for me. He didn't want to know me. I was a disappointment to him. I have realized that what I heard so many years ago was the truth. I was looking at my heavenly Father through the lenses of my experiences with my own father. And for me, that meant my heavenly Father was distant, unavailable, easily disappointed, quick to anger, and often hard to predict. True, I wanted to please him. But since God the Father was, to me, hard to fathom and not especially inviting, my relationship with God centered on my relationship with his Son. Jesus liked me. I wasn't so sure about his Dad.

Daddy, I trust entirely in your love. Despite my human experience, I am convinced that you are a Father who is gracious, generous, warm, and loving.

"If you hold anything against anyone, forgive them."

MARK 11:25

The time has come for us to forgive our fathers and all those who have wounded us. Paul warns us that unforgiveness and bitterness can wreck our lives and the lives of others (Ephesians 4:31; Hebrews 12:15). As someone has said, forgiveness is setting a prisoner free and then discovering the prisoner was you. I found some help in Bly's experience of forgiving his own father, when he said, "I began to think of him not as someone who had deprived me of love or attention or companionship, but as someone who himself had been deprived, by his father and his mother and by the culture."[1] My father had his own wound that no one ever offered to heal. His father was an alcoholic, too, for a time, and there were some hard years for my dad as a young man, just as there were for me. We allow God to bring the hurt up from our past. We acknowledge that it hurt, that it mattered, and we choose to extend forgiveness. This is not saying, "It didn't really matter"; it is not saying, "I probably deserved part of it anyway." Forgiveness says, "It was wrong, it mattered, and I release you." And then we ask God to father us, and to tell us our true name.

Father, as I acknowledge the pain from my past, I make the choice to forgive. It hurt, it mattered, and I choose to extend forgiveness.

Did your earthly father fail to reflect the character of your heavenly one? In what ways? What did you learn from this that helped you grow?

_____

_____

_____

Did your earthly father reflect the character of your heavenly one? In what ways? How did his positive example help mold you in a strengthening way?

_____

_____

_____

What are the ways that your earthly father hurt you? How did this shape who you are today?

_____

_____

Where are you on your journey to forgive?

_____

_____

about HER

The bride belongs to the bridegroom.

JOHN 3:29

ears into my Christian life, I began to hunger to know God more deeply as my Father. I asked him to reveal himself to me as my dad. In answer, God invited me to take a journey deep into my heart that took surprising turns and continues still. First, God led me into taking a much closer look at my own father. Who was he really? How did he really feel about me? What did I even remember? God invited me to go with him into the deep places of my heart that were hidden and wounded and bleeding from heartbreaks and wounds I had received from my father's hand. Places I did not want to go. Memories I did not want to revisit. Emotions I did not want to feel. The only reason I said yes to God, the only reason I would travel there, was because I knew he would go with me. Hand in hand. He would hold my heart. And I had come to trust his. There is a core part of our hearts that was made for Daddy. Made for his strong and tender love. That part is still there, and longing. Open it to Jesus and to your Father God. Ask him to come and love you there. Meet you there. We've all tried so hard to find the fulfillment of this love in other people, and it never works. Let us give this treasure back to the One who can love us best. It is amazing. It is available. Keep pressing in. Keep asking God. And take your heart's question to Jesus. Ask him to show you your beauty. And then? Let him romance you.

....

Daddy, I long for your strong and tender love that you so freely give. Open my eyes to the beauty in me that you see and romance my heart.

"I will give you a new heart and put a new spirit in you."

EZEKIEL 36:26

e may think of God "seeing" us with a sense of guilt—yes, God sees me . . . and what he sees is my sin. That's wrong on two counts. First, your sin has been dealt with. Your Father has removed it from you "as far as the east is from the west" (Psalm 103:12). Your sins have been washed away (1 Corinthians 6:11). When God looks at you he does not see your sin. He has not one condemning thought toward you (Romans 8:1). Not only that, but you have a new heart. That's the promise of the new covenant: "I will give you a new heart and put a new spirit in you; I will remove from you your heart of stone and give you a heart of flesh. And I will put my Spirit in you and move you to follow my decrees and be careful to keep my laws" (Ezekiel 36:26–27). There's a reason that it's called good news. Too many Christians today are living back in the old covenant. They've had Jeremiah 17:9 drilled into them and they walk around believing their heart is deceitfully wicked. Not anymore. Read the rest of the book. In Jeremiah 31:33, God announces the cure for all that: "I will put my law in their minds and write it on their hearts. I will be their God, and they will be my people." I will give you a new heart. That's why Paul said in Romans 2:29, "No, a person is a Jew who is one inwardly; and circumcision is circumcision of the heart, by the Spirit." Sin is not the deepest thing about you. You have a new heart.

....

Thank you, Father, for giving me a new heart. Teach me to see myself as you see me: sinless.

What name do you usually use for God in your conversations?

_____

_____

_____

How does it feel to speak to God with intimate language, like
"Daddy"? Natural or foreign?

_____

_____

_____

When you imagine God noticing you, do you think he's seeing
your sin?

_____

_____

_____

What would it mean in your life if you really believed you've
been given a new heart?

_____

_____

How beautiful you are, my darling!

SONG OF SONGS 1:15

It had been a long, busy day, and I left the boys with John and escaped into the night for some much-needed time alone. I walked along a path toward a park near our home. The air was crisp and clear, the stars winking, glistening. I breathed in the beauty and laid the cares of the day behind me. A cool breeze whispered by, one of the first to speak of the winter to come. As I walked, I was dazzled by the splendor of it all, and I began to compliment God on the great job he had done. "It's beautiful, Lord! The stars are amazing!" *I'm glad you like it, my darling.* I stopped dead in my tracks. I blushed. Did the God of the universe just call me "darling"? I was warmed to the depths of my soul by the endearment, but I also wondered if I had made it up. And was it sacrilegious to believe God would use such a loving name? For me? I am the one who had lost patience with her children that very day and used an ugly tone of voice that hurt them and mortified me. I am the one who is living her life so imperfectly, disappointing friends and failing family. Me? *Darling?* Later that night I read some scriptures before falling asleep, and my hand turned to the pages of the Song of Songs. My eyes fell to the words "How beautiful you are, my darling" (1:15). How kind of God, for then I knew. It had been him. The amazing love of God for me penetrated my heart in a new and deep way that night. He had spoken to me. He loves me as a *lover* loves.

....

Precious Lover of my soul, I hear you calling me darling. Your love penetrates my heart and I receive it as your beloved.

And the God of all grace . . . after you have suffered a little
while, will himself restore you and make you strong.

1 PETER 5:10

rue strength does not come out of bravado. Until we are broken, our lives will be self-centered, self-reliant; our strength will be our own. So long as you think you are something in and of yourself, what will you need God for? I don't want clichés; I want deep, soulful truth. As writer and theologian Frederick Buechner said, "To do for yourself the best that you have it in you to do—to grit your teeth and clench your fists in order to survive the world at its harshest and worst—is, by that very act, to be unable to let something be done for you and in you that is more wonderful still. The trouble with steeling yourself against the harshness of reality is that the same steel that secures your life against being destroyed secures your life also against being opened up and transformed."[1] Only when we enter our wound will we discover our true glory. There are two reasons for this. First, because the wound was given in the place of your true strength, as an effort to take you out. Until you go there, you are still posing, offering something shallower and less substantial. And therefore, second, it is out of your brokenness that you discover what you have to offer the community. The false self is never wholly false. When we begin to offer not merely our gifts but our true selves, that is when we become powerful. That is when we are ready for battle.

....

God, I no longer want to pose before you or others. Help me face my broken-
ness and there discover what you would have me give to others.

Are you comfortable relating to God as a Lover who adores you?

_____

_____

_____

What is the pet name God uses for you?

_____

_____

_____

What are the ways you still see yourself "posing"?

_____

_____

_____

What are the ways you recognize yourself living into your true self?

_____

_____

_____

"Therefore I am now going to allure her."

HOSEA 2:14

A woman becomes beautiful when she knows she's loved. Cut off from love and rejected, a woman wilts like a flower no one waters anymore. She withers into resignation, duty, and shame. The radiance of her countenance goes out, as if a light has been turned off. But this same woman, whom everyone thought was rather plain and unengaging, becomes lovely and inviting when she is pursued. Her heart begins to come alive, come to the surface, and her countenance becomes radiant. Her beauty was always there. What happened was merely the power of romance releasing her true beauty, awakening her heart. She has come alive. As women we long to be loved in a certain way, a way unique to our femininity. We long for romance. We are wired for it; it's what makes our hearts come alive. Somewhere, down deep inside, you know this. But what you might never have known is, this doesn't need to wait for a man.

God longs to bring this into your life himself. He wants to heal us through his love to become mature women who actually know him. He wants us to experience verses like, "Therefore I am now going to allure her; I will lead her into the wilderness and speak tenderly to her" (Hosea 2:14). Our hearts are desperate for this.

....

God, help me to move beyond a childlike receiving of your love to become the mature woman who knows you and loves you.

about HIM

Praise be to the LORD my Rock, who trains my
hands for war, my fingers for battle.

PSALM 144:1

"Dad, are there any castles anymore?" Many years ago Luke and I were sitting at the breakfast table. As soon as he asked the question I knew what his young heart was wondering. Are there any great adventures anymore? Are there any great battles? I wanted to explain that indeed there are, but before I could reply he got this gleam in his eye and asked, "And are there any dragons?" Oh, how deeply this is written into the masculine soul. The boy is a warrior; the boy is his name. A man needs a battle to fight; he needs a place for the warrior in him to come alive and be honed, trained, seasoned. If we can reawaken that fierce quality in a man, hook it up to a higher purpose, release the warrior within, then the boy can grow up and become truly masculine. One day Blaine came downstairs and without a word slipped a drawing he had made in front of me. It was a pencil sketch of an angel with broad shoulders and long hair; his wings were sweeping around him as if just unfurled to reveal that he was holding a large two-handed sword. He held the blade upright, ready for action, his gaze steady and fierce. Beneath the drawing were the words, written in the hand of a nine-year-old boy, "Every man is a warrior inside. But the choice to fight is his own." He knew as deeply as he knew anything that every man is a warrior, yet every man must choose to fight.

....

Warrior God, show me the battle that has my name on it so that the warrior in me might come alive and be honed, trained, and seasoned.

What would it be like to experience for yourself that the truest thing about your love's heart toward yours is not disappointment or disapproval but deep, fiery, passionate love?

_____

_____

_____

How would knowing this change your life?

_____

_____

_____

Looking back to when you were a boy, where do you now recognize your thirst for adventure?

_____

_____

Where in your life are you embracing the adventurous warrior inside you?

_____

_____

about HER

"I looked at you and saw that you were old enough for love."

EZEKIEL 16:8

ou might recall that Scripture often uses metaphors to describe our relationship with God. We are portrayed as clay, and he is the potter. We are sheep, and he the shepherd. Each metaphor is beautiful and speaks to the various seasons of our spiritual lives and to the various aspects of God's heart toward us. But have you noticed they ascend in a stunning way? From potter and his clay to a shepherd and his sheep, there is a marked difference in intimacy, in the way they relate. It gets even better. From master and servant to father and child, there is a wonderful progression into greater intimacy. It grows more beautiful when he calls us his friends. But what is most breathtaking is when God says he is our Lover (our Bridegroom), and we are his bride. That is the pinnacle, the goal of our redemption and the most intimate of all. God has been wooing you ever since you were a little girl. Yes, we said earlier that the story of your life is the story of the long and sustained assault upon your heart by the one who knows what you could be and fears you. But that is only part of the story. Every story has a villain. Every story also has a hero. The Great Love Story the Scriptures are telling us about also reveals a Lover who longs for you. The story of your life is also the story of the long and passionate pursuit of your heart by the One who knows you best and loves you most.

....

Bridegroom, I am yours and you are mine. I long for you just as you long for me, and I am grateful for your passionate pursuit of my heart.

about HIM

"Whoever loses their life for me and for the gospel will save it."

MARK 8:35

A man must have a battle to fight, a great mission to his life that involves and yet transcends even home and family. He must have a cause to which he is devoted even unto death, for this is written into the fabric of his being. Listen carefully: you do. That is why God created you—to be his intimate ally, to join him in the Great Battle. You have a specific place in the line, a mission God made you for. That is why it is so essential to hear from God about your true name, because in that name is the mission of your life. "I'd love to be William Wallace, leading the charge with a big sword in my hand," sighed a friend. "But I feel like I'm the guy back there in the fourth row, with a hoe." That's a lie of the Enemy—that your place is insignificant, that you aren't armed for battle. There is no other man who can replace you in your life, in the arena you've been called to. If you leave your place in the line, it will remain empty. No one else can be who you are meant to be. You are the hero in your story. Not a bit player, not an extra, but the main man. This is the next leg in the initiation journey, when God calls a man forward to the front lines. He wants to develop and release in us the qualities every warrior needs—including a keen awareness of the enemies we will face. Above all else, a warrior has a vision; he has a transcendence to his life, a cause greater than self-preservation.

Mighty God, I reject the lie that my place is insignificant and that I am unarmed. Show me the arena into which you're calling me to be the hero, and I will go.

How hard or easy is it for you to imagine God as the Bridegroom who adores you?

_____

_____

_____

If you truly received that goodness, what would be different in your life?

_____

_____

_____

Can you relate to the guy who feels like he's in the fourth row with a hoe? How?

_____

_____

_____

What is the arena into which God is calling you?

_____

_____

about HER

For great is his love toward us.

PSALM 117:2

*W*hen John told me the story of God allowing him to see a massive humpback whale, impossibly close to shore, he knew it was a gift from God to his heart alone, a gift from the Lover of his heart. And as happy as I was for him, I was hungrier for such a kiss for myself. I wanted to experience God's love for me, personally. Soon after, I sat on the sand, looked out to the sea, and asked God for a whale. "I know you love John, Jesus, but do you love me too? That much? If you do, may I have a whale too?" I felt a little silly in asking, for I knew the truth—that God had already proven his love for me. He had sent his only Son, Jesus, to die for me (John 3:16). He had rescued me. He had paid the highest price imaginable for me. The northern coast of California is rocky, and as I picked my way through, I rounded a corner and came upon a beautiful orange starfish. And I knew at once it was God's gift to me, his kiss. He didn't give me a whale; no, that was for John alone. For me, unique to me, he gave a stunning starfish. He answered my question. He loved me. I thanked him for it, then rounded the next bend and came upon a sight I will never forget. There before me, behind me, surrounding me, were hundreds of starfish. There were purple ones and orange ones and blue ones, all sizes. I burst into joyful laughter, my heart exploding inside me. God didn't just love me. He *loooved* me! Intimately, personally, completely.

. . . .

God, I receive your love for me that is intimate, personal, and complete! Thank you for being the Lover of my heart.

I am not really the one doing wrong; it is sin living in me that does it.

ROMANS 7:20 NLT

*E*ver since that fateful day when Adam gave away the essence of his strength, men have struggled with a part of themselves that is ready at the drop of a hat to do the same. We don't want to speak up unless we know it will go well, and we don't want to move unless we're guaranteed success. What the Scriptures call the flesh, the old man, or the sinful nature, is that part of fallen Adam in every man that always wants the easiest way out. It's much easier to go down to the driving range and attack a bucket of balls than it is to face the people at work who are angry at you. It's much easier to clean the garage, organize your files, cut the grass, or work on the car than it is to have a difficult or uncomfortable conversation. To put it bluntly, your flesh is a weasel, a poser, and a selfish pig. And your flesh is not the real you. When Paul gives us his famous passage on what it's like to struggle with sin (Romans 7), he tells a story we are all too familiar with. But what Paul concludes is just astounding: "I am not really the one doing wrong; it is sin living in me that does it" (Romans 7:20 NLT). Did you notice the distinction he makes? Paul says, "Hey, I know I struggle with sin. But I also know that my sin is not me—this is not my true heart." You are not your sin; sin is no longer the truest thing about the man who has come into union with Jesus. Your heart is good.

....

Gracious God, I confess that I've agreed with the lie that my flesh is the real me. I reject the lie and agree with you that my heart is good.

Can you relate to the longing for God to give you a special gift, just for you?

_____

_____

_____

When have you recognized God's tender personal love for you?

_____

_____

_____

How does your sinful flesh most often get the best of you? How have you found ways to change your perception and see the truth?

_____

_____

_____

Why does it matter that your flesh is *not who you are*?

_____

_____

Create in me a pure heart, O God.

PSALM 51:10

I live a life much like yours—full of demands, pressures, and disappointments. Like you, there are seasons in my life when Jesus seems very near and seasons where I can't seem to find him at all. Sometimes it feels like we're playing a game of hide-and-seek, but he's got all the best hiding places staked out. All relationships ebb and flow. The ebbing is to draw our hearts out in deeper longing. In the times of emptiness, an open heart *notices*: What are you feeling? Like a lonely girl missing her daddy? Like a young woman feeling completely invisible, unseen? Often God allows these feelings to surface to help us remember times when we have felt like this before. Notice how you handle your heart. Are you shutting down in anger? Turning to food? To others? What is crucial is that *this* time we handle our hearts differently. We ask our Lover to come for us, and we keep our eyes and our hearts open to his coming. We choose not to shut down. We let the tears come. We allow the ache to swell into a longing prayer for our God. And he comes, dear hearts. He does come. The times of intimacy—the flowing waters of love—those times then bring healing to places in our hearts that still need his touch. An intimate relationship with Jesus is not only for other women, for women who seem to have their acts together, who appear godly. It is for each and every one of us. God wants intimacy with *you*.

....

God, you allow my heart to notice what's going on inside when I'm lonely or lost or afraid. Thank you for the intimacy that you and I share.

Be strong and courageous.

DEUTERONOMY 31:6

tart choosing to live out your strength and you'll discover that it grows each time. Rich was after some brakes for his car; he called the parts store and they quoted him a price of fifty dollars for the pair. But when he got down there, the guy told him it would be ninety dollars. Something in Rich was provoked. Normally he would have said, "Oh, that's okay. It's no big deal," and paid the higher price; but not this time. He told the guy that the price was fifty dollars and stood his ground. The guy backed down. "It felt great," Rich told me later. "I felt that I was finally acting like a man." Now, that may seem like a simple story, but this is where you will discover your strength, in the daily details of your life. Begin to taste your true strength and you'll want more. Something in the center of your chest feels weighty, substantial. We must let our strength show up. It seems so strange, after all this, that a man would not allow his strength to arrive, but many of us are unnerved by our own masculinity. What will happen if we really let it out? Our strength is wild and fierce, and we are more than unsettled by what may happen if we let it arrive. One thing we know: nothing will ever be the same. One client said to me, "I'm afraid I'll do something bad if I let all this show up." No, the opposite is true. You'll do something bad if you don't. Remember—a man's addictions are the result of his refusing his strength.

Ferocious God, I confess that I've avoided exercising my strength in my daily life. Today I choose to express strength you give!

When you're having big feelings, are you quick to notice and acknowledge them?

_____

_____

_____

What prayer practice can help you offer those feelings to God?

_____

_____

_____

Did you relate to Rich, who stood up to the mechanic? Why or why not?

_____

_____

_____

When was the last time you exercised your fierce strength in a healthy way?

_____

_____

about HER

You have stolen my heart with one glance of your eyes.

SONG OF SONGS 4:9

hat is it that God wants from you? He wants the same thing that you want. He wants to be loved. He wants to be known as only lovers can know each other. He wants intimacy with you. Yes, he wants your obedience, but only when it flows out of a heart filled with love for him. "Whoever has my commands and keeps them is the one who loves me" (John 14:21). Following hard after Jesus is the heart's natural response when it has been captured and has fallen deeply in love with him. You've probably heard that there is in every human heart a place that God alone can fill. But George MacDonald said that there is also in God's heart a place that you alone can fill. You. You are meant to fill a place in the heart of God no one and nothing else can fill. He longs for you. You are the one who overwhelms his heart with just "one glance of your eyes" (Song of Songs 4:9). You are the one he sings over with delight and longs to dance with across mountaintops and ballroom floors (Zephaniah 3:17). You are the one who takes his breath away by your beautiful heart that, against all odds, hopes in him. Let that be true for a moment. Let it be true of you. God wants to pour his love into your heart, and he longs to have you pour yours into his. He wants your deep heart, that center place that is the truest you.

....

Beloved, I long to be intimate with you. I receive the truth that there is a place in your heart that only I can fill!

A man's heart reveals the man.

PROVERBS 27:19 NKJV

hat is this enemy that the Scripture calls "the world"? Is it drinking and dancing and smoking? Is it going to the movies or playing cards? That is a shallow and ridiculous approach to holiness. It numbs us to the fact that good and evil are much more serious. No, "the world" is not a place or a set of behaviors—it is any system built by our collective sin, all our false selves coming together to reward and destroy each other. Take all those posers out there, put them together in an office or a club or a church, and what you get is what Scripture means by "the world." The world is a carnival of counterfeits—counterfeit battles, counterfeit adventures, counterfeit beauties. Men should think of it as a corruption of their strength. Battle your way to the top, says the world, and you are a man. Why is it, then, that the men who get there are often the emptiest, most frightened, prideful posers around? They are mercenaries, battling only to build their own kingdoms. There is nothing transcendent about their lives. The same holds true of the adventure addicts; no matter how much you spend, no matter how far you take your hobby, it's still merely that—a hobby. The world offers a man a false sense of power and a false sense of security. Where does your own sense of power come from? Consider what you would think of yourself if tomorrow you lost everything that the world has rewarded you for. Jesus warns us against anything that gives a false sense of power.

....

Father God, I confess that I've accepted the counterfeits the world offers, and that they have corrupted my strength. Forgive me.

When you think of offering God the most intimate part of yourself, how does that feel?

_____

_____

_____

When and where do you spend that intimate time with God?

_____

_____

_____

What are the specific ways you've accepted the world's counterfeits?

_____

_____

_____

If tomorrow you lost everything that the world has rewarded you for, what would you think of yourself?

_____

_____

"She has done a beautiful thing to me."

MARK 14:6

here was an event that took place in the life of Jesus that he said should be told whenever the gospel is proclaimed around the world. It was when Mary of Bethany came and anointed him with the perfume, which cost a year's wages. It was an extravagant act of sacrificial worship, and the aroma of it filled the room. Jesus was profoundly moved by it. Though the men gathered there were indignant, Jesus said, "She has done a beautiful thing to me." It was a woman who did this for Christ. Just as it was also a woman who rushed into the Pharisee's house uninvited and washed Jesus' feet with her tears, dried them with her hair, and kissed them in an act of intimate, repentant worship. It was women who followed Jesus from Galilee to care for his needs. It was women who stayed at the foot of the cross, offering him the comfort of their presence until he breathed his last. It was to women that Jesus first revealed himself after he rose from the dead. Women hold a special place in the heart of God. A woman's worship brings Jesus immense pleasure and a deep ministry. You can minister to the heart of God. You affect him. You matter. Jesus desires you to pour out your love on him in extravagant worship. This is not just for women who have the time, women who are really spiritual. You are made for romance, and the only one who can offer it to you consistently and deeply is Jesus. Offer your heart to him.

....

God, I pour out my love in heartfelt worship to you! Show me how to love you in extravagant ways.

We are not unaware of his schemes.

2 CORINTHIANS 2:11

The devil no doubt has a place in our theology, but is he someone we even think about in the daily events of our lives? Has it ever crossed your mind that not every thought that crosses your mind comes from you? We are being lied to all the time. Yet we never stop to say, "Wait a minute . . . who else is speaking here? Where are those ideas coming from?" If you read the saints from every age you'll find that they take the devil very seriously indeed. As Paul said, "We are not unaware of his schemes" (2 Corinthians 2:11). But we, the enlightened, have a much more commonsense approach to things. We look for a psychological or physical or even political explanation for every trouble we meet. Who caused the Chaldeans to steal Job's herds and kill his servants? Satan, clearly (Job 1:12, 17). Yet do we even give him a passing thought when we hear of terrorism today? Who kept that poor woman bent over for eighteen years, the one Jesus healed on the Sabbath? Satan, clearly (Luke 13:16). But do we consider him when we are having a headache that keeps us from praying or reading Scripture? Who moved Ananias and Sapphira to lie to the apostles? Satan again (Acts 5:3). But do we really see his hand behind a fallout or schism in ministry? Who was behind that brutal assault on your own strength, those wounds you've taken?

....

Great God, I have fallen victim to the enemy's brutal assault on my strength. Heal my wounds and open my eyes to his schemes.

How are you like or unlike Mary of Bethany?

_____

_____

_____

What is the extravagant worship Jesus wants from you?

_____

_____

_____

Are you in the habit of noticing the Enemy's work in your life?
Why or why not?

_____

_____

_____

What would change if God opened your eyes to increasingly
notice Satan's wily ways?

_____

_____

_____

> *Come, let us bow down in worship.*
>
> PSALM 95:6

*G*etting time with your First Love is worth whatever it costs. Ask his help in making you desperately hungry for him. Ask his help in creating the time and space you need to draw close to him. Ask him to come, to reveal himself to you as the Lover that he is. Go get some worship music that moves you. Music that draws you into intimacy with him. Go to a private place. Turn off your phone. Bring your Bible and a journal to write down what you hear God say in the depths of your heart. Kneel, sit, or lie down and ask the Holy Spirit to come and help you worship Jesus. Start by telling Jesus how wonderful he is. Remember when he took care of that hard situation? Or that time he answered your prayers for financial help? Recall the times he spoke to you in your loneliness or need. Thank him for being so faithful. Stay. Linger. Worship. Let the music usher your heart into God. Singing along with songs that proclaim his worthiness helps our spirit come into alignment with the truth of these words whether we feel them to be true or not. The first time may not be amazing. You may think your words and cries are bouncing off the ceiling. We grow in this as we practice. We practice the presence of God. We come to God in worship not to *get* from him but to give to him. Jesus loves it when we offer our hearts to him in devotion.

....

My Love, my heart's desire, you are worthy of all my praise. With unbridled devotion, I offer you my whole heart.

Pray continually.

1 THESSALONIANS 5:17

Before an effective military strike can be made, you must take out the opposing army's line of communication. The Evil One does this all the time—in ministries and especially with couples. Marriage is a stunning picture of what God offers his people. The Enemy knows this, and he hates it with every ounce of his malicious heart. He has no intention of just letting that beautiful portrait be lived out before the world with such deep appeal. So just like in the Garden, Satan comes in to divide and conquer. I'll feel this sense of accusation when I'm with my wife. It's hard to describe, but I just receive this message that I'm blowing it. When I brought this up with Stasi, tears came to her eyes. "You're kidding," she said. "I've been feeling the very same thing. I thought you were disappointed with me." *Wait a minute,* I thought. *If I'm not sending this message and you're not sending this message . . .* Most of all the Enemy will try to jam communications with Headquarters. Commit yourself to prayer every morning for two weeks and just watch what happens. Many times I've come under a cloak of confusion so thick I suddenly find myself wondering why I ever believed in Jesus in the first place. That sweet communion I normally enjoy with God is cut off. If you unaware, you'll think you really have lost your faith or been abandoned by God or whatever lie the Enemy tells you.

....

Holy Spirit, open my eyes to the schemes of the Evil One. Be my helper when communication fails, with you or with my wife.

Was there once a boyfriend that you couldn't wait to spend time with? Who? What about him created such a desire?

_____

_____

_____

Do you have that passion for time with God? If not, ask him to birth it in your heart.

_____

_____

_____

How has your communication been with your wife lately?

_____

_____

_____

How has your communication with God been?

_____

_____

_____

The LORD, the LORD himself, is my strength.

ISAIAH 12:2

We long for the protection masculine strength offers. To have them shield us from physical harm, yes. But also to have them shield us from emotional harm and spiritual attack. To intercede for us in a relationship that has become hurtful. A friend was repeatedly being verbally abused and manipulated by her mother over the phone. Finally, her husband took the phone and spoke to her mother. "You cannot talk to my wife this way. I will not allow it. You may not call again until you are ready to be kind." He did for her what she was unable to do for herself. As women we sometimes long for someone strong to stand between us and the vicious assaults of our Enemy. One weary night I had gone to bed early, overcome with a sense of despair and hopelessness. I felt pounded down, beyond saving, and worthy of condemnation. Suddenly, John was at my bedside. He was angry, but not at me. He recognized the hand of our Enemy. He began to forcefully command the minions of Satan to release me; he commanded them to be silent, and he sent them to the throne of Jesus for judgment. As he continued to pray for me, I began to feel lighter. When he finished, tears were streaming down my face and my hands were raised to God in holy gratitude and joyful worship. Strength is what the world longs to experience from a man.

....

Jesus, I admit that I desperately long for someone to stand between me and the vicious assaults of our Enemy. Be my shield and empower my husband to protect me.

about HIM

For the accuser of our brothers and sisters . . . has been hurled down.

REVELATION 12:10

The Enemy is constantly broadcasting messages to try to demoralize us. Propaganda. After all, Scripture calls him the "accuser of our brethren" (Revelation 12:10 NKJV). Think of what goes on—what you hear and feel—when you really blow it. *I'm such an idiot; I always do that; I'll never amount to anything.* Sounds like accusation to me. How about when you're really trying to step forward as a man? I was driving to the airport for a trip to the West Coast, to give a talk to men about *Wild at Heart.* All the way there I was under this cloud of heaviness; I was nearly overcome by a deep sense of *John, you're such a poser. You have absolutely nothing to say. Just turn the car around, go home, and tell them you can't make it.* Now, in my clearer moments I know it's an attack, but you must understand that all this comes on so subtly it seems true at the time. I nearly gave in and went home. When Christ is assaulted by the Evil One in the wilderness, the attack is ultimately on his identity. "If you are the Son of God," Satan sneers three times, then prove it (Luke 4:1–13). I had a dream where I was accused of committing adultery; I hadn't, but in my dream no one would believe me. Hear this: so long as a man remains no real threat to the Enemy, Satan's line to him is *You're fine.* But after you do take sides, it becomes *Your heart is bad and you know it.*

....

Holy God, open my eyes to see the ways that the Enemy is causing mayhem through his lies and chaos. May I be a threat to his power.

When has a man stepped in to protect you, verbally or physically?

_____

_____

_____

Where do you feel most under attack? Where do you feel most supported?

_____

_____

_____

When have you recognized Satan's disruption in your life?

_____

_____

_____

What are the spiritual tools you have to fight the deceiver's chaos?

_____

_____

about HER

Let the king be enthralled by your beauty.

PSALM 45:11

eauty is what the world longs to experience from a woman. We know that. Most of our shame comes from this knowing and feeling that we have failed here. Beauty is an essence that dwells in every woman. It was given to her by God. It was given to you. Surely you would agree that God is nothing if not beautiful. All around us God's creation shouts of his beauty and his goodness. The silhouette of lace on a bare tree draped with ice, the rays of sun streaming forth from a billowing cloud, the sound of a brook trickling over smooth stones, and the form of a woman's body all speak of God's good heart if we will have the eyes to see. God's beauty is lavished on the world. Beauty may be the most powerful thing on earth. Beauty *speaks*. Beauty *invites*. Beauty *nourishes*. Beauty *comforts*. Beauty *inspires*. Beauty is *transcendent*. Beauty draws us to God. God has given this Beauty to Eve, to every woman. Beauty is core to a woman—who she is and what she longs to be—and is one of the most glorious ways we bear the image of God in a broken and often ugly world. Women are creatures of great mystery; not problems to be solved but mysteries to be enjoyed. And that, too, is part of her glory. The only things standing in the way of our beauty are our doubts and fears, and the hiding and striving we turn to as a result.

....

God who is my Maker, I embrace the beauty you have imbued in my core.
May it speak, invite, nourish, comfort, and inspire through me.

"Watch and pray so that you will not fall into temptation."

MATTHEW 26:41

The Enemy probes the perimeter, looking for a weakness. Satan will throw a thought or a temptation at us in hopes that we will swallow it. He knows your story, knows what works with you, and so the line is tailor-made to your situation. This morning he attacked my prayer time. If I thought this was all me, I'd be very discouraged. Knowing that my heart is good allowed me to block it, right then and there. When Satan probes, make no agreements. You'll see a beautiful woman and something in you will say, You want her. That's the Evil One appealing to the traitor within. If the traitor says, Yes, I do, then the lust really begins to take hold. This can become a stronghold and make a good man feel so awful because he thinks he's a lustful man when he's not; it's an attack through and through. Now, I'm not blaming everything on the devil. In almost every situation there are human issues involved. Every man has his struggles; every marriage has its rough spots; every ministry has personal conflicts. But those issues are like a campfire that the Enemy throws gasoline all over and turns into a bonfire. The flames leap up into a raging inferno and we are suddenly overwhelmed with what we're feeling. All the while we believe that it's us, that we're to blame, and the Enemy is laughing because we've swallowed the lie . We've got to be a lot more cunning than that.

....

God, open my eyes to recognize the ways the Enemy's schemes are tripping me up. I reject his lie and stand on your truth.

Where do you notice beauty in yourself?

_____

_____

_____

How does that beauty bless others?

_____

_____

_____

When the Enemy probes your perimeter, where does he find
weakness? Where does he find strength?

_____

_____

_____

What is the lie the deceiver most often uses on you? How can
you take this lie apart by applying the truth?

_____

_____

_____

You shall be a crown of beauty in the hand of the LORD.

ISAIAH 62:3 ESV

ou see, beauty indwells every woman. We've seen it so many times, counseling women of all ages. Like a shy doe, it reveals itself for a moment, then fades back into cover. Usually it comes when she doesn't know it, when she isn't trying to make it come. Rather, something is happening that allows her defenses to come down for a moment. For instance, when someone is listening. She knows that she matters. Someone cares about her heart, wants to know her. Her beauty emerges as if from behind a veil. So the choice a woman makes is not to conjure beauty but to let her defenses down. Beauty comes with it. A woman in her glory, a woman of beauty, is a woman who is not striving to become beautiful or worthy or enough. *She knows in her quiet center where God dwells that he finds her beautiful, has deemed her worthy, and in him, she is enough.* In fact, the only thing getting in the way of our being fully captivating and enjoyed is our striving. "He will quiet you with His love" (Zephaniah 3:17 NKJV). A woman of true beauty is a woman who in the depths of her soul is at rest, trusting God because she has come to know him to be worthy of her trust. She exudes a sense of calm, a sense of rest, and invites those around her to rest as well. She speaks comfort; she knows that we live in a world at war, that we have a vicious enemy, and our journey is through a broken world. But she also knows that because of God all is well, that all will be well.

....

Lover of my heart, in my quiet center where you dwell, I agree that you find me beautiful and have deemed me worthy. In you, I am enough.

Above all else, guard your heart.

PROVERBS 4:23

In any hand-to-hand combat, there's a constant back-and-forth of blows, dodges, blocks, counterattacks, and so forth. That's exactly what is going on in the unseen around us. Only it takes place, initially, at the level of our thoughts. When we are under attack, we've got to hang on to the truth. This is how Christ answered Satan—he didn't get into an argument with him, try to reason his way out. He simply stood on the truth. He answered with Scripture and we've got to do the same. Satan doesn't just throw a thought at us; he throws feelings too. Walk into a dark house late at night and suddenly fear sweeps over you; or just stand in a grocery line with all those tabloids shouting sex at you and suddenly a sense of corruption is yours. But this is where your strength is revealed and even increased—through exercise. Stand on what is true and do not let go. Period. When Proverbs 4:23 tells us to guard our hearts, it's not saying, "Lock them up because they're really criminal to the core"; it's saying, "Defend them like a castle, the seat of your strength you do not want to give away." As Thomas à Kempis said, "Yet we must be watchful, especially in the beginning of the temptation; for the enemy is then more easily overcome, if he be not suffered to enter the door of our hearts, but be resisted without the gate at his first knock."[1]

....

Father, I recognize that I am vulnerable to Satan's schemes, and I choose to stand on what is true. Be my helper!

On a scale of "belief" to "disbelief," where do you land when it comes to believing that you reflect God's beauty?

_____

_____

_____

Are you able to agree that in God all is well, and all will be well? Why or why not?

_____

_____

_____

What's the temptation that Satan knows you'll likely fall for?

_____

_____

_____

In very practical terms, how do you protect yourself from succumbing to this temptation?

_____

_____

Taste and see that the L ORD is good.

PSALM 34:8

Many years ago our family was staying with friends at their little cabin in an old mountain town in Colorado. One morning as we drove to a remote area where we planned to take a hike, we passed a home that was surrounded by a garden of stunning beauty. Groves of towering delphiniums, profuse foxgloves, clematis and roses caught my eyes and my heart. Later that day I returned. I needed to get closer to that garden. I wanted to immerse myself in its extravagance. Emboldened by my desire, I walked up to the front door and knocked. A small, elderly woman answered the door and eyed me with suspicion. I quickly introduced myself as a visitor who had seen her garden, been completely captured by it, and wondered if I could walk around in it. Her wariness melted into delight. She came out to show me the garden herself, and we spent a wonderful afternoon together. Beauty beckons us. Beauty invites us. *Come, explore, immerse yourself.* God—Beauty himself—invites us to know him. "Taste and see that the L ORD is good" (Psalm 34:8). He delights in alluring us and in revealing himself to those who wholeheartedly seek him. He wants to be known, to be explored. A woman does too. She fears it, but below the fear is a longing to be known, to be seen as beautiful and enjoyed. So the unveiled beauty of a woman entices and invites.

....

Lord, you promise to reveal yourself to those who wholeheartedly seek you. Unveil your beauty, as I do the same.

Resist the devil, and he will flee from you.

JAMES 4:7

hen we begin to question the Enemy, to resist his lies, to see his hand in the "ordinary trials" of our lives, then he steps up the attack; he turns to intimidation and fear. Satan will try to get you to agree with intimidation because he fears you. You are a huge threat to him. He doesn't want you waking up and fighting back, because when you do he loses. "Resist the devil," James says, "and he will flee from you" (4:7). So he's going to try to keep you from taking a stand. He moves from subtle seduction to open assault. The thoughts come crashing in, things begin to fall apart in your life, your faith seems paper thin. Why do so many pastors' kids go off the deep end? You think that's a coincidence? So many churches start off with life and vitality only to end in a split, or simply wither away and die. How come? Why did a friend of mine nearly black out when she tried to share her testimony at a meeting? Why are my flights so often thwarted when I'm trying to take the gospel to a city? Because we are at war and the Evil One is trying an old tactic—strike first and maybe the opposition will turn tail and run. He can't win, you know. As Franklin Roosevelt said, "The only thing we have to fear is fear itself."[1]

·····

Dear Heavenly Father, you have opened my eyes to the devil's schemes, and I commit to resisting him in your mighty name.

Beauty beckons us. Who do you know who is like the welcoming gardener who wants to share her bounty?

_____

_____

_____

What in your life brings you delight when you share it with others?

_____

_____

_____

When was a time when you were doing God's work and felt the Enemy's interference?

_____

_____

_____

What scripture emboldens you most to stand firm?

_____

_____

Work out your salvation with fear and trembling.

PHILIPPIANS 2:12

woman who is hiding invites others to do the same. A woman who makes herself vulnerable and available for intimacy invites others to do the same. After all, Eve is the incarnation of the heart of God for intimacy. She says to the world, through her invitation to relationship, "You are wanted here. We want to know you. Come in. Share yourself. Be enjoyed. Enjoy me as I share myself." A woman who is controlling cannot invite others to rest, to be known. They will feel controlled in her presence. It won't feel safe there. *A woman who is unveiling her beauty is inviting others to life.* She risks being vulnerable; exposing her true heart and inviting others to share theirs. She is not demanding, but she is hopeful. When our assistant Cherie walks into the room, it feels as if someone has just opened the windows and let the fresh air in. She offers her beauty by asking good questions and by sharing something of her times with God—an insight, a glimpse into his heart. She entices others to the heart of God. Ultimately, a woman invites us to know God. To experience through her that God is merciful and tender and kind. That God longs for us—to be known by us and to know us. She invites us to experience that God is good, deep, lovely, alluring. Captivating. Here is where we "work out" our salvation as God works in us (Philippians 2:12–13).

....

Lord Jesus, make me a woman who is unveiling my beauty and inviting others to life!

> *Put on the full armor of God, so that you can take*
> *your stand against the devil's schemes.*
>
> EPHESIANS 6:11

gainst the flesh, the traitor within, a warrior uses discipline. We have a two-dimensional version of this now, which we call a "quiet time." But most men have a hard time sustaining any sort of devotional life because it has no vital connection to recovering and protecting their strength; it feels about as important as flossing. But if you saw your life as a great battle and you knew you needed time with God for your very survival, you would do it. Maybe not perfectly, but you would have a reason to seek him. We give a half-hearted attempt at the spiritual disciplines when the only reason we have is that we ought to. But time with God each day is not about academic study or getting through a certain amount of Scripture. It's about connecting with God. Sometimes I'll listen to music; other times I'll read Scripture or a passage from a book; often I will journal. Then there are days when all I need is silence and solitude and the rising sun. The point is simply to do whatever brings me back to my heart and the heart of God. God has spared me many times from an ambush I had no idea was coming; he warned me in my time with him in the early morning about something that was going to happen that day. The whole point is connecting with God. If you do not have God and have him deeply, you will turn to other lovers.

....

Father God, I thirst to be with you and to hear from you. Quicken my heart to long deeply for time with you.

In what ways do you relate to the woman who is hiding?

_____

_____

_____

In what ways do you relate to the woman who is controlling?

_____

_____

_____

In what ways has your time with God grown stale?

_____

_____

_____

What are practical ways to invigorate the time you spend with God?

_____

_____

_____

_____

They make it a place of springs.

PSALM 84:6

We do not always get what we want, but that doesn't mean that we no longer want. It means we stay awake to the unmet longing and ache. To possess true beauty, we must be willing to suffer. I don't like that. Yet, if Christ himself was perfected through his sufferings, why would I believe God would not do the same with me? Women who are stunningly beautiful are women who have had their hearts enlarged by suffering. By paying the high price of loving truly and honestly without demanding that they be loved in return. They have come to know that when everyone and everything has left them, God is there. They have learned, along with David, that those who go through the desolate valley will find it "a place of springs" (Psalm 84:6). Living in true beauty can require much waiting, much time, much tenacity of spirit. We must constantly direct our gazes toward the face of God, even in the presence of longing and sorrow. It is in the waiting that our hearts are enlarged. The waiting does not diminish us. God does not always rescue us out of a painful season. He does not always give to us what we so desperately want when we want it. He is after something much more valuable than our happiness. He is restoring and growing in us an eternal weight of glory. And sometimes . . . it hurts.

Lord, you know the ways that I am hurting, and I trust you with my heart. Restore and grow in me an eternal weight of glory, even when it hurts.

There is a friend who sticks closer than a brother.

PROVERBS 18:24

on't even think about going into battle alone. Don't even try to take the masculine journey without at least one man by your side. Yes, there are times a man must face the battle alone, in the wee hours of the morn, and fight with all he's got. But don't live a lifestyle of isolation. The church understands now that a man needs other men, but what we've offered is another two-dimensional solution: accountability groups or partners. But we don't need accountability groups; we need fellow warriors, someone to fight alongside, someone to watch our back. The whole crisis in masculinity today has come because we no longer have a warrior culture, a place for men to learn to fight like men. We don't need a meeting of Really Nice Guys; we need a gathering of Really Dangerous Men. That's what we need. Yes, we need men to whom we can bare our souls. But it isn't going to happen with a group of guys you don't trust, who really aren't willing to go to battle with you. It's a long-standing truth that there is never a more devoted group of men than those who have fought alongside one another, the men of your squadron, the guys in your foxhole. It will never be a large group, but we don't need a large group. We need a band of brothers willing to shed their blood with us.

God, surround me with other men who will watch my back as we fight alongside one another for what matters most.

Who is a woman you know who is beautiful because of her suffering?

_____

_____

_____

In what ways have you suffered to reflect true beauty? How has this strengthened you?

_____

_____

_____

Who are the men in your band of brothers?

_____

_____

_____

If you are alone, what are the reasons you have chosen to be alone? Who is one man to whom you can reach out this week?

_____

_____

Love one another deeply, from the heart.

1 PETER 1:22

nveiling our beauty really just means unveiling our feminine hearts. It's scary, for sure. That is why it is our greatest expression of faith, because we are going to have to trust Jesus. We'll have to trust him that we *have* a beauty, that what he has said of us is true. And we'll have to trust him with how it goes when we offer it, because that is out of our control. We'll have to trust him when it hurts, and we'll have to trust him when we are finally seen and enjoyed. That's why unveiling our beauty is *how* we live by faith. Unveiling our beauty is our greatest expression of hope. We hope there is a greater and higher Beauty, hope we are reflecting that Beauty, and hope it will triumph. And we unveil beauty in the hope that Jesus is *growing* our beauty. No, we are not yet what we long to be. But we are underway. Restoration has begun. To offer beauty now is an expression of hope that it will be completed. And unveiling beauty is our greatest expression of love because it is what the world most needs from us. When we choose not to hide, when we choose to offer our hearts, we are choosing to love. Jesus offers; he invites; he is present. That is how he loves. That is how we love. Our focus shifts from self-protection to the hearts of others. We offer Beauty so that their hearts might come alive, be healed, know God. That is love.

....

God, teach me to unveil beauty in hope. I am not yet what I long to be, but I am confident that my restoration has begun because of and through you.

Rescue the weak and the needy;
deliver them from the hand of the wicked.

PSALM 82:4

nce upon a time there was a beautiful maiden, an absolute enchant-
ress. Whether the daughter of a king or a common servant girl, she
was a princess at heart. Her flowing hair, her deep eyes, her luscious lips,
her sculpted figure—the sun was pale compared to her light. Her heart was
golden, her love as true as an arrow. But this lovely maiden was unattain-
able, the prisoner of an evil power who held her captive in a dark tower.
Only a champion could win her; only the most valiant, daring, and brave
warrior could set her free. And then, against all hope he comes; with cunning and raw courage he lays siege to the tower and the sinister one who
holds her. Three times the knight is thrown back, but three times he rises
again. Finally, the sorcerer is defeated; the dragon falls; the giant is slain.
The maiden is his; through his valor he has won her heart. On horseback
they ride off into the sunset. Why is this story so deep in our psyche? Every
little girl dreams that one day her prince will come. And one day the boy,
now a young man, realizes that he wants to be the one to win the beauty.
From ancient fables to the latest blockbuster, the theme of a good man win-
ning the heart of a good and beautiful woman is universal to human nature.
It is written in our hearts, one of the core desires of man and woman.

....

Creator God, who knit me together in the womb, you know the deepest
longings of my heart. Empower me to be the one to win the Beauty!

When have you made a bold choice not to hide?

_____

_____

_____

Who is Jesus calling you to love?

_____

_____

_____

When have you lived into the role of the brave hero?

_____

_____

_____

How is God calling you to live into this good story?

_____

_____

_____

_____

He'll validate your life in the clear light of day.

PSALM 37:6 MSG

No man can tell you who you are as a woman. No man declares the verdict on your soul. One woman said to us, "I still feel useless. I am not a woman. I do not have a man. I have failed to captivate someone." The ache is real. But the verdict is false. Only God can tell you who you are. Only God can speak the answer you need to hear. That is why we spoke of the romance with him first. It comes first. It must. It has to. Adam is a far too unreliable source! Now, yes, in a loving relationship, we are meant to speak to each other's wounds. In love we can bring such deep joy and healing as we offer to each other our strength and beauty. It means the world for John to have me say, "You are such a man." And it means the world to me to have John say, "Stasi, you are a beautiful woman." We can—and should—offer this to each other. This is one way our love helps to heal our mate's wound. But our *core* validation, our *primary* validation has to come from God. And until it does, until we look to him for the healing of our souls, our relationships are hurt by looking to each other for something only God can give. No matter how much Adam pours into your aching soul, it's never enough. He cannot fill you. Maybe he's pulled away because he senses you're asking him to fill you. Every woman has to reckon with this—this ache she tries to get her man to fill. To learn how to love him, you must first stop insisting that he fill you.

....

Lord, I turn my eyes toward you—and away from human men—to receive my core validation. You are the one in whom I find my life.

about HIM

He will take great delight in you.

ZEPHANIAH 3:17

Just as every little boy is asking one question, every little girl is as well. But her question isn't so much about her strength. No, the deep cry of a little girl's heart is, *Do you see me? Am I worth choosing, worth fighting for? Am I lovely?* Every woman needs to know that she is exquisite and exotic and chosen. This is core to her identity, the way she bears the image of God. *Will you pursue me? Do you delight in me? Will you fight for me?* I am not saying every woman needs a man to be complete. I am saying every woman wants to be loved, romanced, part of a shared adventure. And like every little boy, she has taken a wound as well. The wound strikes right at the core of her heart of beauty and leaves a devastating message with it: No. You're not beautiful and no one will fight for you. Like your wound, hers almost always comes at the hand of her father. A little girl looks to her father to know if she is lovely. The power he has to cripple or to bless is just as significant to her as it is to his son. If he's a violent man he may even defile her verbally or sexually. A girl's heart is violated and the message is driven further in: you are not desired for your heart; you will not be protected; no one will fight for you. The tower is built brick by brick, and when she's a grown woman it can be a fortress.

....

Father, teach me to be a friend to women. Show me how to affirm the value of my wife and of other women, for your glory.

From what men have you sought validation?

_____

_____

_____

As you tip your ears toward God's voice, what do you hear him whispering to you?

_____

_____

_____

Was your wife wounded by her earthly father? If so, how?

_____

_____

_____

Are there practical ways in which you can minister to that hurt?

_____

_____

_____

_____

about HER

Your beauty ... should be that of your inner self.

1 PETER 3:3–4

esolate women don't attack or dominate. But neither do they allure. Their message is simply, "There's nothing here for you." A man in her presence feels . . . uninvited. Unwanted. It's a form of rejection, emasculation to be sure. However, resentful women can be softened. Timid women can gain a sense of self. And in doing so, they become alluring. The effect on the men in their lives is astounding. What severity and domineering and hiding and whining could not do, beauty does. Their men come forth as good men, repentant men. Heroes. An alluring woman is one who calls forth the best in a man by offering who she is as a woman—someone who offers her beauty, her true heart. And then there's the woman who is not arousing. She is manipulating and demanding. However it is expressed in the uniqueness of your own femininity, arousing Adam comes down to this: *Need him. And believe in him.* That is what a man needs to hear from his woman more than anything else. *I need you. I need your strength. I believe in you. You have what it takes.*

....

Lord, heal the rough places where I am desolate so that my husband might know he is invited and wanted by me.

The tongue has the power of life and death.

PROVERBS 18:21

There is something mythic in the way a man is with a woman. Our sexuality offers a parable of amazing depth when it comes to being masculine and feminine. The man comes to offer his strength and the woman invites the man into herself, an act that requires courage and vulnerability and selflessness for both of them. Notice first that the man must move; his strength must swell before he can enter her. But neither will the love consummate unless the woman opens herself in stunning vulnerability. When both are living as they were meant to live, the man enters his woman and offers her his strength. She draws him in, embraces and envelops him. When all is over, he is spent; but ah, what a sweet death it is. And that is how life is created. The beauty of a woman arouses a man to be the man; the strength of a man, offered tenderly to his woman, allows her to be beautiful; it brings life to her and to many. This is far more than sex. It is a reality that extends to every aspect of our lives. When a man withholds himself from his woman, he leaves her without the life only he can bring. This is never truer than with how a man offers—or does not offer—his words. Life and death are in the power of the tongue, says Proverbs 18:21. She is made for and craves words from him.

....

Father, empower me to show up for my beloved in a way that elicits the woman you made her to be.

Do you *need* your husband? Why or why not?

_____

_____

_____

Do you *believe in* your husband? Why or why not?

_____

_____

_____

Are there ways you fail to show up for your wife? If so, what are they?

_____

_____

_____

How do you show up for her?

_____

_____

_____

_____

> *"And the two will become one flesh."*
>
> MARK 10:8

The way femininity can awaken masculine strength—and the way a good man's strength allows a woman to be beautiful—can be offered in all sorts of holy ways between men and women not married to one another. Far too long we have lived in a culture of fear in the church, worrying that any relationship between men and women will end in an affair. Sadly, we have forsaken so many opportunities to call one another forth with the grace of our genders. There are all sorts of opportunities for this. It will be unavoidable. As a man comes alive, the women in his world will experience and enjoy his strength, the power of his masculine presence. As a woman comes alive, the men in her world will experience and enjoy her beauty, the richness of her feminine presence. Yes—this exchange of strength and beauty will be a test of character. When something is awakened in us by another man or woman, we do have a choice in that moment. We choose to accept the awakening as an invitation to go find that with *our* man or woman. Or to pray, if we are single, that this sort of man or woman will come to us from God's hand. We will *have* to face this kind of test as we relate to members of the opposite sex. Remember our answer to the question, "How do I love a man?" This is a principle, a picture of how femininity can encourage masculinity in many ways.

....

Lord, heal me and equip me to awaken the masculine strength of my husband so that he might experience and enjoy the richness of my feminine presence.

They will be called oaks of righteousness.

ISAIAH 61:3

Heroes are willing to die to set others free. This sort of heroism is what we see in the life of Joseph, the husband of Mary and the earthly father to Jesus Christ. I don't think we've fully appreciated what he did. Mary, an engaged young woman, ends up pregnant, claiming: "I'm carrying God's child." The situation is scandalous. What is Joseph to think; what is he to feel? Hurt, confused, betrayed no doubt. But he's a good man; he will simply "divorce her quietly" (Matthew 1:19).

An angel comes to him in a dream to convince him that Mary is telling the truth and he is to follow through with the marriage. This is going to cost him. Imagine what he'll endure if he marries a woman the whole community thinks is an adulteress. He will be shunned by his business associates and most of his clients; he will certainly lose his standing in society and his place in the synagogue. Notice the insult that crowds will later use against Jesus. "Isn't this Joseph and Mary's son?" they say with a sneer and a nudge and a wink. In other words, we know who you are—an illegitimate child. Joseph will pay big-time for this move. Does he withhold? No, he offers Mary his strength; he steps right between her and all that mess and takes it on. He spends himself for her. Isaiah announces, "They will be called oaks of righteousness" (Isaiah 61:3). There, under the shadow of a man's strength, a woman finds rest.

....

*Lord of Hosts, mighty Rescuer, make me the kind of hero—like Christ—
who is willing to die to set others free.*

How are you intentional about awakening your husband's masculinity?

_____

_____

_____

In what ways can you grow in this area?

_____

_____

_____

It took courage for Joseph to show up for Mary. Do you know a man like this, who risks to love well? How does this man's example affect you?

_____

_____

_____

In what ways do you love your wife well?

_____

_____

"They will be divided . . . mother against daughter
and daughter against mother."
LUKE 12:53

We are not all mothers, but we all had one. Or longed for one. The relationship between a mother and daughter is a holy, tender, fierce thing. The desire in a daughter to please her mother is matched only by her desire to be separate from her. Most mother/daughter relationships go through a stormy season during the girl's adolescence. Words are flung, accusations aimed at the heart. The way a mother weathers this stormy season of her daughter's transition from girlhood to womanhood can affect their relationship for the rest of their lives. Many a good woman makes the desperate mistake of believing that her daughter is a reflection of herself, an extension of herself, and therefore the verdict on her as a mother and as a woman. She is dumbfounded, disappointed, sometimes wounded deeply when her "little girl" makes choices wholly foreign to what she would have chosen. This can be deeply wound the relationship. Girls' hearts flourish in homes where they are *seen* and *invited* to become ever more themselves. Parents who enjoy their daughters are giving them and the world a great gift. Mothers in particular have the opportunity to offer encouragement to their daughters by inviting them into their feminine world and by treasuring their daughters' unique beauty.

....

Father God, you know exactly what my relationship with my mother was
like. I offer it to you and ask you to touch my wounded places.

Fight the good fight of the faith.

1 TIMOTHY 6:12

*W*ill you fight for her? That's the question Jesus asked me many years ago, right before our tenth wedding anniversary, right at the time I was wondering what had happened to the woman I married. I knew what he was saying—stop being a nice guy and act like a warrior. Play the man. I brought flowers, took her to dinner, and began to move back toward her in my heart. But I knew there was more. That night, before we went to bed, I prayed for Stasi in a way I'd never prayed for her before. Out loud, before all the heavenly hosts, I stepped between her and the forces of darkness that had been coming against her. I didn't really know what I was doing, only that I needed to take on the dragon. Everything we've learned about spiritual warfare began that night. And you know what happened? Stasi got free; the tower of her depression gave way as I began to truly fight for her. And it's not just once, but again and again over time. That's what really stumps us. Some men are willing to go in once, twice, even three times. But a warrior is in this for good. A friend is in the middle of a very hard, very unpromising battle for his wife. It's been years now without much progress and without much hope. With tears in his eyes, he said to me, "I'm not going anywhere. This is my place in the battle. This is the hill that I will die on." His wife may respond or she may not. That's really no longer the issue. The question is simply: *What kind of man do you want to be?*

....

God who fights for those who are bound, make me the man who will fight for my wife. Equip me with strength to be your warrior.

How did your mother affirm you as a woman?

_____

_____

_____

In what ways might she have done better in affirming you?

_____

_____

_____

How do you step between your wife and the forces of darkness?

_____

_____

_____

Is there a way, this week, that you can love her in this way?
How?

_____

_____

_____

_____

about HER

> *Train a child in the way he should go, and when*
> *he is old he will not depart from it.*
>
> PROVERBS 22:6 NKJV

s large as the role is that our mothers play, the word *mother* is more powerful when used as a verb than as a noun. All women are not mothers, but all women are called to *mother*. As daughters of Eve, all women are uniquely gifted to help others in their lives become more of who they truly are—*to encourage, nurture, and mother them toward their true selves*. In doing this, women partner with Christ in the vital mission of bringing forth life. "Train a child in the way he should go, and when he is old he will not depart from it" (Proverbs 22:6 NKJV). This verse is not a promise about faith. It is not speaking of training a child to follow Christ or promising that if you do, the grown child will continue to follow him. It is about raising a child to know who he is and to guide him in becoming ever more himself. *In the way he should go*. It speaks of teaching a child to live from his heart, attuned to it, awake to it, aware of it, and when that child is grown he will continue to live a life from the heart. *It is about seeing who a person really is and calling him out to be that person*. The impact on a life that has been seen and called out is dramatic and eternal. The nurturing of life is a high and holy calling. And as a woman, it is yours. Yes, it takes many shapes and has many faces. Uniquely and deeply, this calling makes up part of the very fiber of a woman's soul—the calling to mother.

....

Father, I offer myself to nurture life so others might grow healthy and strong.

Live as free people.

1 PETER 2:16

Cliff jumping is one of our family favorites. Jumping Rock is perched above the river at about the height of a two-story house plus some, tall enough that you can slowly count to five before you hit the water. There's something that makes every cliff seem twice the height when you're looking down from the top and everything in you says, Don't even think about it. So you don't think about it, you just hurl yourself off and plunge into the cold water. When you come back up the crowd is cheering and something in you is also cheering because you did it. We all jumped that day, first me, then Stasi, Blaine, Sam, and even Luke. Then some big, hulking guy who was going to back down once he saw what the view was like from above—but he had to jump because Luke did it and he couldn't live with himself knowing he'd cowered while a six-year-old boy hurled himself off. After that first jump, you have to do it again—partly because you can't believe you did it and partly because the fear has given way to the thrill of such freedom. I want to live my whole life like that. I want to love with more abandon and stop waiting for others to love me first. I want to hurl myself into a creative work worthy of God.

....

God, teach me to love with more abandon and stop waiting for others to love me first. Today I hurl myself into a creative work worthy of you!

When you were a girl, did you look forward to being a mother?
In what ways?

_____

_____

_____

How is God speaking to you about your capacity to nurture
others?

_____

_____

_____

Have you stood at a height, gathering your courage to jump?
When and where?

_____

_____

_____

Is there a risk into which God is inviting you? How is it a risk?

_____

_____

Where you go I will go, and where you stay I will stay.

RUTH 1:16

love the way female friends are with each other. When I gather with a group of friends, inevitably someone begins to rub someone else's back. Hair gets played with. Merciful, tender, caressing, healing touches are given. Men don't do this with each other. It is unique to women. When women gather, they ask meaningful questions. They want to know how you are. Women friends unabashedly dive into matters of the heart. My mom mothered me. But she isn't the only woman who has. My sisters certainly did, as well as elementary school teachers and neighbors. These days I receive it from the gentle, tender acts of kindness offered to me from the friends God has given me. The gift of friendship among women is a treasure not to be taken lightly. Women friends become the face of God to one another—the face of grace, of delight, of mercy. The capacity of a woman's heart for meaningful relationships is vast. A woman must have women friends. Ruth was speaking to a woman when she said, "Where you go I will go, and where you stay I will stay. Your people will be my people and your God my God" (Ruth 1:16). Our friendships flow in the deep waters of the heart where God dwells and transformation takes place. It is here, in this holy place, that a woman can partner with God in influencing another and *being influenced* by another for lasting good. It is here that she can mother, nurture, encourage, and call forth Life.

....

Father God, you know the longing of my heart for deep relationships with women. Teach me to befriend others and to grow deep with them.

"I have come that they may have life, and have it to the full."

JOHN 10:10

G il Bailie, founder and president of the Cornerstone Forum, shared a piece of advice given to him some years back by a spiritual mentor, Howard Thurman: "Don't ask yourself what the world needs. Ask yourself what makes you come alive, and go do that, because what the world needs is people who have come alive."[1] I was struck dumb. Suddenly my life up until that point made sense in a sickening sort of way; I realized I was living a script written for me by someone else. All my life I had been asking the world to tell me what to do with myself. This is different from seeking counsel or advice; what I wanted was freedom from responsibility and especially freedom from risk. I wanted someone else to tell me who to be. Thank God it didn't work. The scripts they handed me I simply could not bring myself to play for very long. Like Saul's armor, they never fit. Can a world of posers tell you to do anything but pose yourself? As Buechner said, we are in constant danger of being not actors in the drama of our lives but reactors, "to go where the world takes us, to drift with whatever current happens to be running strongest."[2] Reading the counsel Thurman gave to Bailie, I knew it was God speaking to me. It was an invitation to come out of Ur. I set the volume down without turning another page and went to find a life worth living.

....

Dear Heavenly Father, I trust you will guide me and teach me how to live a life that is authentic to the man you've created me to be.

Are you satisfied with your female friendships? Why or why not?

_____

_____

_____

What is one step you can take, this week, to reach out and show love to a friend?

_____

_____

_____

What is it that makes you come alive?

_____

_____

_____

How are you living into that today?

_____

_____

_____

_____

about HER

> *"Greater love has no one than this: to lay down one's life for one's friends."*
>
> JOHN 15:13

ittle girls have best friends. Grown women long for them. To have a woman friend is to relax into another soul and be welcomed in all that you are and all that you are not. To know that as a woman, you are not alone. Friendships between women provide a safe place to share in the experiences of life *as a woman*. Who but another woman can fully understand mammograms, the longing to bear a child, and living in a world that feels run by men? It is a great gift to know that you see as another sees, an immense pleasure to be understood, to enjoy the easy companionship of one with whom you can let your guard down. Friendship is a great gift. One to be prayed for and not taken for granted. If you do not have the kind of friendship you long for, ask God to bring it into your life, to give you eyes to recognize it when he does. When God gives a friend, he is entrusting us with the care of another's heart. It is a chance to mother and to sister, to be a Life giver, to help someone else become the woman she was created to be, to walk alongside her and call her deep heart forth. Friendships need to be nurtured and guarded and fought for. We need to call one another without waiting to be called first. We need to ask how our friends are doing and really listen to their answers. Listen between the lines. We love our friends by *pursuing* them—calls, gifts, cards, invitations to chat or go for a walk. We offer our hearts.

....

Lord, I thank you for my female friends and ask you to teach me how to love them well so that they might flourish.

"What will it profit a man if he gains the whole world, and loses his own soul?"

MARK 8:36 NKJV

Where would we be today if Abraham had carefully weighed the pros and cons of God's invitation and decided that he'd rather hang on to his medical benefits, three weeks paid vacation, and retirement plan in Ur? What would have happened if Moses had lived a careful, cautious life steering clear of all burning bushes? You wouldn't have the gospel if Paul had concluded that the life of a Pharisee was at least predictable and certainly more stable than following a voice he heard on the Damascus road. Where would we be if Jesus was not fierce and wild and romantic to the core? Come to think of it, we wouldn't be at all if God hadn't taken that enormous risk of creating us in the first place. Most men spend the energy of their lives trying to eliminate risk, or squeezing it down to a more manageable size. If it works, if a man succeeds in securing his life against all risk, he'll wind up in a cocoon of self-protection and wonder why he's suffocating. If it doesn't work, he curses God and redoubles his efforts. When you look at the structure of the false self that men tend to create, it always revolves around two themes: seizing upon some sort of competence and rejecting anything that cannot be controlled. But you sacrifice your soul and your true power when you insist on controlling things.

....

Forgive me, God, for the ways I've secured my life against risk. Teach me to live like Jesus: fiercely, and wildly, and romantic to the core!

Who is the friend who initiates most frequently with you? Is there anything you can learn from her?

_____

_____

_____

Who is the friend to whom you most often reach out first? What have you learned from this relationship?

_____

_____

_____

Where are you living safely and cautiously?

_____

_____

_____

Where is God inviting you to take a risk today?

_____

_____

_____

Be devoted to one another in love.

ROMANS 12:10

*L*et me say clearly, true friendship is *opposed*. One woman often feels less important to the other, or accused or needy or misunderstood. Honest communication in love is the only way to live and grow in friendships. There are ebbs and flows. There may be real hurt and disappointment. In fact, it's inevitable in our broken world. But with the grace of God firmly holding us, reminding us that he is the source of our true happiness, it is possible to nurture and sustain deep friendships throughout our lives. We are designed to live in relationship and share in the lives of other women. We need each other. God knows that. But for a woman to enjoy relationship, she must repent of her need to control and her insistence that people fill her. Fallen Eve demands that people "come through" for her. Redeemed Eve is being met in the depths of her soul by Christ and is free to offer to others, free to desire, and willing to be disappointed. Fallen Eve has been wounded by others and withdraws to protect herself from further harm. Redeemed Eve knows that she has something of value to offer, that she is made for relationship. Therefore, being safe and secure in her relationship with her Lord, she can risk being vulnerable with others and offer her true self.

....

Lord, because you are redeeming me, you've met me in the depths of my soul and have freed me to offer to others, freed me to desire, and even freed me to be disappointed.

"I will put breath in you, and you will come to life."

EZEKIEL 37:6

Too many men forsake their dreams because they aren't willing to risk, fear they aren't up to the challenge, or are never told that those desires deep in their hearts are good. But the soul of a man isn't made for controlling things; it's made for adventure. When God set man on the earth he gave us an incredible mission—a charter to explore, build, conquer, and care for all creation. God never revoked that charter. It's still there, waiting for a man to seize it. If you had permission to do what you really want to do, what would you do? Don't ask how. *How* is never the right question; *how* is a faithless question. It means "unless I can see my way clearly, I won't believe it, won't venture forth." *How* is God's department. He is asking you what. *What is written in your heart? What makes you come alive?* If you could do what you've always wanted to do, what would it be? You see, a man's calling is written on his true heart, and he discovers it when he enters the frontier of his deep desires. To paraphrase Thurman's advice to Gil Bailie, don't ask yourself what the world needs; ask yourself what makes you come alive, because what the world needs are men who have come alive. A man's life becomes an adventure, the whole thing takes on a transcendent purpose when he releases control in exchange for the recovery of the dreams in his heart.

....

As I offer myself to you, Lord, nurture in my heart a spirit ready to explore, build, conquer, and care for all of creation.

What was the last hard conversation you had with a friend? How did the conversation unfold?

_____

_____

_____

What is the hard conversation you need to have with a friend?

_____

_____

_____

Are you living out that thing written on your heart, your unique purpose?

_____

_____

_____

What next step do you need to take to be the man God made you to be?

_____

_____

His bride has made herself ready.

REVELATION 19:7

adies, you are the Bride of Christ—and the Bride of Christ is a warring bride. Often the hardest person to fight for is . . . yourself. But you must. Your heart is *needed*. You must be present and engaged in order to love well and fight on behalf of others. Without you, much will be lost. It is time to take a stand and to stand firm. We are at war. You are needed. Yes, men are created in the image of the Warrior King. Men are warriors. But women need to fight too. It is a powerful good when a man battles for a woman's heart and stands between her and her enemies. But often, there is not a man present in a woman's life to fight on her behalf. And even when there is, God desires the woman's spirit to rise up in his strength as well. And men need women to engage in spiritual warfare on their behalf. One day we will be queens—we will rule with Jesus (Revelation 21). We need to grow in our understanding and practice of spiritual warfare not only because we are being attacked but because it is one of the primary ways that we grow in Christ. He uses spiritual warfare in our lives to strengthen our faith, to draw us closer to him, to train us for the roles we are meant to play, to encourage us to play those roles, and to prepare us for our future at his side. It is *not* that we are abandoned. Christ has not abandoned us. It is *not* that we are alone. He will never leave us or forsake us. It is *not* even up to us. The battle is the Lord's.

....

Lord, I am ready to battle for you. Make me the mighty spiritual warrior who strengthens others' faith and draws them closer to you.

about HIM

*"I have called you friends, for everything that I learned
from my Father I have made known to you."*

JOHN 15:15

here comes a time in a man's life when he's got to head off into the unknown with God. This is a vital part of our journey, and if we balk here, the journey ends. Before the moment of Adam's greatest trial, God provided no step-by-step plan, gave no formula for how he was to handle things. That was not abandonment; that was the way God honored Adam. What God did offer Adam was friendship. He wasn't left alone to face life; he walked with God in the cool of the day and there they talked about what lessons he was learning and what adventures were to come. This is what God is offering to us as well. The only way to live in this adventure—with all its danger and unpredictability and immensely high stakes—is in an ongoing, intimate relationship with God. The control we so desperately crave is an illusion. Far better to give it up in exchange for God's offer of companionship. Abraham knew this; Moses did as well. Read through the first several chapters of Exodus—it's filled with a give-and-take between Moses and God. They knew each other, like they really were intimate allies. David—a man after God's own heart—also walked and warred and loved his way through life in a conversational intimacy with God. This is the way every comrade and close companion of God lives. God calls you his friend. He wants to talk to you—personally, frequently.

God, make me a man after your own heart. As I walk with you, be my intimate companion.

In what ways are you doing battle in prayer for others?

_____

_____

_____

How might God be calling you to wage war?

_____

_____

_____

How is your conversation with God going these days? Can it be improved? If so, how?

_____

_____

_____

What is the time and place where you can be most intimate with God?

_____

_____

_____

NOTES

Day 18

   1. Robert Bly, *Iron John: A Book About Men, 25th Anniversary Edition* (Philadelphia: Da Capo Press, 2015), 98.

Day 20

   1. C. S. Lewis, *Perelandra* (New York: Scribner, 2003), 172.

Day 23

   1. Henry Wadsworth Longfellow, *Prose Works of Henry Wadsworth Longfellow* (Boston: Ticknor and Fields, 1857), 1:452.

Day 25

   1. William Blake, "Proverbs of Hell," in *The Marriage of Heaven and Hell* (Boston: John W. Luce & Co., 1906), 15.

Day 27

   1. George MacDonald, *Unspoken Sermons Series I, II, and III* (New York: Start Publishing [1867] 2012), 27–28.

   2. George McDonald, "The New Name," in *Unspoken Sermons Series I, II, and III* (Project Gutenberg [1867] 2015), www.gutenberg.org/ebooks/9057.

Day 34

   1. Neil T. Anderson, *The Bondage Breaker* (Eugene: Harvest House Publishers [1990] 2006), 224–25.

Day 35

1. Robert Bly, *Iron John: A Book About Men*, 25th Anniversary Edition (Philadelphia: Da Capo Press, 2015), 25.

Day 37

1. Frederick Buechner, *The Sacred Journey: A Memoir of Early Days* (New York: HarperCollins [1982] 1991), 46.

Day 47

1. Thomas à Kempis, *Of the Imitation of Christ* (New York: D. Appleton & Co., 1844), 39.

Day 48

1. Franklin D. Roosevelt, "Inaugural Address, March 4, 1933," in *The Public Papers and Addresses of Franklin D. Roosevelt*, ed. Samuel I. Rosenman, vol. 2, *The Year of Crisis, 1933* (New York: Random House, 1938), 11.

Day 57

1. Howard Thurman quoted in Gil Bailie, *Violence Unveiled: Humanity at the Crossroads* (New York: Crossroad, 1995), xv.
2. Frederick Buechner, *The Longing for Home: Recollections and Reflections* (New York: HarperCollins, 1996), 109.

SCRIPTURE INDEX

Scriptures Used in Alphabetical Order